DEC 15 /2012

DEC 15 /2012

MW01103685

HE WHO LAUGHS, LASTS

FOR Cathy

who Always feels
Like extended family
AND to LISA too
Best To you Both
for the New Year

ALSO BY JOSH FREED

Moonwebs

A 21st Century Survival Guide (with Terry Mosher)

The Anglo Guide to Survival in Qubec (with Jon Kalina)

Sign Language and Other Tales of Montreal Wildlife

Vive le Québec Freed!

Fear of Frying and Other Fax of Life

Press One and Pray and Other Letters from Voice Jail

HE WHO LAUGHS, LASTS

JOSH FREED

Véhicule Press

Published with the assistance of the Canada Council for the Arts, the Canada Book Fund of the Department of Canadian Heritage, and the Société de développement des entreprises culturelles du Québec (SODEC).

Cover design: David Drummond
Typeset in Minion and MrsEaves by Simon Garamond
Printed by Marquis Printing Inc.

ISBN: 978-1-55065-346-5

Published by Véhicule Press, Montréal, Québec, Canada
www.vehiculepress.com

Distribution in Canada by LitDistCo
www.litdistco.ca

Distributed in the U.S. by Independent Publishers Group
www.ipgbook.com

Printed in Canada on recycled paper

Contents

Preface

There's only one antidote to our speed-crazed, tech-obsessed, pass-word-plagued, financially-jittery, fitness-fetishist, gluten-sensitive, fatness-fearing world—and that's to laugh at it.

That's what I try to do every Saturday in my weekly column for the Montreal *Gazette*—a satirical effort that ranges from occasionally funny with scattered chuckles to frequently funny with odd storms of laughter.

This is my first collection of columns in twelve years. Since these stories first appeared in the newspaper they've been polished, updated and re-written by sophisticated computer robots to suit changing times, avoid lawsuits and regulate laughter within acceptable 21st century social norms.

Several stories in this book poke fun at how technology is transforming our way of life, in a world where "iPhone therefore I am"—and you'd better say "I AGREE" or your contract with me is cancelled. Others look at our growing health obsession in a society where we're consumed by what we consume. For every new study that says something is good for you, there's an equal and opposite study that says it isn't.

Many stories are about urban life in my own city, Montreal, which is just like other cities only more so. It has more potholes, more jaywalkers, more collapsing bridges, more student protests and more chaos than most places—but it also has more passion, craziness and soul. And I think, more laughter.

There's a series of stories about Canadians—God's Frozen People—battling to survive in the icebox of North America, the land of the freeze. Other stories look at our inter-connected new global world that seems under constant threat of catastrophe from everything from West Nile virus, Asian bird flu and mad cow disease to terrorist shoe-bombers, trans-fat-loaded cereals and the ancient Mayan's supposed death sentence on our whole planet.

The Four Horsemen of the Apocalypse have become 400.

All this is best faced with humor. The late American newspaper columnist, Hallam Walker Davis once said: "A good columnist is forever flipping things upside down and wrong side up and inviting us to look and laugh .... and maybe even think." And that's what I try to do, at least on Saturdays.

Studies show that laughter adds several years to your life, so take two pages of this book each morning—and you'll live longer. This book is recommended by pharmacists!

Thanks to my unofficial editor Stephen Phizicky who faithfully calls me every week to throw around ideas, since he knows my brain works better in dialogue than monologue. Thanks also to friends Victor Dabby, Jon Kalina and Janet Torge for their ideas—as well as *Gazette* Managing Editor Catharine Wallace, for her frequent last-minute suggestions. Also to Simon Dardick at Véhicule Press for his help in realizing this book.

Finally thanks to my wife Ingrid Peritz, a talented writer whose sharp eye and inquiring mind play a part in almost everything I write. She's the woman behind my smile.

joshfreed49@gmail.com

I

iPhone Therefore I Am

A Plague of Passwords

To read this column, please answer the following security questions:

What was your second grade teacher's first pet's name?
What is your favorite color?
What is my favorite color?

I was travelling recently and dropped in at an Internet cafe. But when I tried to get my e-mail, I was struck by a terrifying modern disease: password amnesia. I couldn't recall which password I used for my Hotmail. Was it joshf or jfreed? Or freedjosh?

No—that was my Indigo book club password! Or was it my barbershop gold card code?

At home, my computer automatically stores all my passwords, but while travelling, I have to remember them—and they'd blurred into a jumble after two weeks away. Like a hacker trying to break into someone's computer, I took a few educated guesses. I tried my street name, then my son's name, then my wife's birthday. I also tried the top-secret code I have for banking—but what the heck did I change that to last time I lost my card? My grandmother's maiden name, backwards? Or my height in centimeters followed by my age when I took piano lessons?

The fact is we all suffer from occasional password amnesia—because we have too many passwords. We used to need a secret password or number for serious security matters like credit cards, Swiss bank accounts and automatic garage doors. But now everyone insists we have one, in a plague of passwords. I need passwords for my hotmail and gmail, bank cards and phone cards, phone plans and Aeroplans. I have passwords for Apple, Amazon, Fido, eBay, iTunes, Indigo, Ticketmaster, the Rogers Cup, the Grey Cup and Second Cup.

Just to hear my own phone messages in my own home I must

punch in *98 and then my security password. Who am I protecting myself against? Is there a wave of burglars breaking into houses and ransacking voice mail boxes? "Hey Lefty—forget the diamonds! They've got phones messages!"

Most people have one high-security password for important stuff and one low-security password they can easily recall—usually their street name, their child's name or their hamster's name. But many sites have strict rules and reject your password if it doesn't have ten letters and include a number, a capital letter and an umlaut. So you have to modify your password slightly. Then, when you log in you can't remember which version to use: josh1, josh9 or josh with an umlaut?

Type your password incorrectly three times and you'll get your account suspended and have to talk to Password Control as they try to "verify your identity." They'll ask you security questions about your first middle school, your second husband and your last mistress. Then they'll make you "reset" your password with a new one—and suddenly you've got something else to forget.

Meanwhile I'm asked for new passwords every week by book clubs, travel sites and Internet dry cleaning companies. Should I give them all the same code and leave myself vulnerable to some six-year-old hacker—or keep inventing new codes and leave myself vulnerable to me?

Choosing new passwords is getting harder too because we're running out of easy ones. For the *New York Times*, even five years ago, I had to settle for the user name joshf49—the closest thing to my name available back then—but now you'd be lucky to get joshf287853. Billions of people may soon face a worldwide password shortage and end up with such obscure 45-letter passwords they'll spend their lives answering security questions about their fifth goldfish.

We interrupt this column for a security check. An unauthorized user may be on this page trying to read this story and your mind, in an attempt to steal your password to knittingworld.com. Please answer the following security questions:

What was the name of your neighbor's hamster?
What do these letters say: Zcbgx5 &^$#—in Greek?
What is your bank PIN number?

Another hoop we must now jump through is deciphering weird distorted letters onscreen that we must re-type correctly. For instance, if you want to email someone a curry recipe from gourmetrecipes. com, you first have to identify blurry letters that seem to spell "ypoletka brezhnev."

It's a bit like an eye doctor chart but harder to read, so I usually fail and must try another set of letters that looks like "grfzuhs cereal" —and I fail again and decide I don't want to email that recipe anyway. I'm told these eye exams are to prove we are humans, not computers that are programmed to constantly scan the net trying to steal everyone's identity. Apparently machines can't read these distorted letters, so by deciphering them we prove we are people. So why do I feel like I'm being turned into a machine instead?

Why do we need so much security anyway? Are we a nation of secret agents? The average person now has more secret passwords than the Allied Supreme Commander did during World War II.

Is this really necessary? Are we living in a dangerous electronic world where we're constantly at risk of having our identity robbed if we don't change our Pizza World password every ninety days?

Or are we just victims of a paranoid overzealous security system that's developed a life of its own by wasting ours? Whatever the answer, I suspect it will only get worse. Soon our microwaves, toasters and blenders will all require passwords too. After we have been verified by Visa we will be re-verified by "Verified by Verified by Visa."

It won't be long before computers learn to read those distorted letters too—and we'll need new and more profound ways to prove we're human. Before signing into childrenstampworld.ca we will have to answer complex emotional questions about Hamlet's relationship with his mother.

Then my stove will lock me out and demand a password based

on recipes only I could know? "Please answer this question: What temperature do you use to bake your mother's famed lasagna casserole?"

Frankly, I dream of a day when I have one universal code tattooed on my ear, or my rear. Sure, someone may break into all my systems and listen to my phone calls, then read my junk mail—but I don't really mind, as long as they answer it all too. I'm tired of living like a secret agent, since I don't really have that many secrets. Except for my Hotmail password—whatever that is.

If you enjoyed this column please complete the following Reader Satisfaction Survey. To use it, simply decipher the following security message only an actual human can see:

We are sorry—you failed to decipher the message. Please contact security. Otherwise security will contact you.

Dear Esteemed Friend

As a columnist I receive lots of emails from Canadians, but lately I've been inundated by hundreds of letters from exotic places like Nigeria and Burkina Faso. The writers are obviously big fans of mine, because they offer me many kind words and the chance to share in "A FORTUNE IN U.S. DOLLARS AND GOLD BULLION!!"

Their letters usually start with a warm greeting like "DEAR FRIEND," or "ESTEEMED SIR," then go on to tell long, fascinating stories in frequent bursts of capital letters.

"I AM MATTHEW UDEBE, son of the late Minister of Mines of Sierra Leone," begins a typical missive. "My father was massacred by President Injani Kabbah's forces during the rebel struggle, but before he died he left his family OVER $35 MILLION IN DIAMONDS AND 40 KILOS OF GOLD BULLION!!"

Matthew hopes to share this sum with a "RELIABLE AND REPUTABLE CHRISTIAN FOREIGNER" like me, who can help transfer the funds out of his country—and if I could simply provide minor small details about myself and my bank account, my bullion is practically in the mail.

Many letters come from Nigeria, where emails are rumored to be the top national export. But I've also gotten generous offers from Prince Joe Ebohli of Ouagadougou, as well as the mistress of former Congo president Laurent Kabila, who both want to share around $20 million with me.

It seems handwritten confidence schemes were common for decades in these countries and have now been passed on, like an ancient family skill to a young computer-literate generation who dominate the global letter-writing market. The astonishing thing is that my letters are almost never the same. Each is a unique essay, written in its own flowery words, in English right out of David Copperfield. I feel like Uriah Heep is writing to me:

GOOD DAY, KIND FRIEND!! MAY I CRAVE YOUR
INDULGENCE TO SOLICIT YOUR CO-OPERATION
FOR A BUSINESS OPPORTUNITY, THAT WILL SURELY
BRING US GOD'S BLESSING!!!

As I read these long-winded, long-distance pleas, I picture the
writers dressed in dusty white jackets and pounding away on battered
Underwoods—and I try to conjure them up. Do they work alone
from their small village homes like individual craftsmen? Or do they
use "HOW-TO-MAKE-A-MILLION-ON-NIGERIAN-EMAIL" form
letters that they get at their local post office, where you just fill in
your name-and-tragedy, along with all the exclamation marks you
want.

Is it possible that all the writers are working together in one
enormous room, thousands of them, like a busy Indian call center—
on long rows of computers where the CAPITAL LETTER KEY IS
PERMANENTLY LOCKED ON under company policy?

How do these writers all come my way? I'm known as a soft
touch with panhandlers on my block, but how did my reputation
spread as far as Lagos? And how many letters do they send out to
people like me to get one response? 10 million? Or 10 billion? Does
anyone ever answer?

Apparently so—since police say North Americans are reportedly
bilked out of tens of millions of dollars each year by similar letters.
But reading these remarkable pieces of storytelling, it's hard to
believe anyone takes them seriously. We live in a world of global
communications, global cuisine, global pollution and global scam
artists—and we all have to do some filtering to separate the goods
from the hoods.

Frankly, I rarely get letters from Ouagadougou and I'm eager to
know more. So yesterday, I wrote back to Prince Ebohli, doing my
best to learn from his writing style.

GREETINGS PRINCE!
I AM JOSHUA NKOMO FREED, PRESIDENT OF

THE PEOPLE'S REVOLUTIONARY COMMITTEE OF ESPLANADE STREET. I received your communication with formidable enthusiasm!

"Before I endeavor to move forward with your proposition, in the interest of friendship I would humbly request to know a great deal more information about yourself, your homeland, your vegetation and crops, your natural resources and of course your august ancestral lineage. Then we can arrange the modalities of our fund transfer.

Yours faithfully, with GOD'S BLESSING!!

I await my next letter eagerly. I mean, you never know—I recently saw a *New Yorker* cartoon showing two guys on a huge yacht, with one asking the other how he made his fortune.

"Easy," he replies. "I answered an email from Nigeria."

Let's Bleep the Beep

Uh-oh. Something in the house is beeping—but what? Is it the stove announcing that dinner is cooked, or the dryer proclaiming my clothes are ready? Is the fridge defrosting, the thermostat adjusting, the smoke alarm dying—or is my cellphone dead? I live in an electronic jungle where I'm been trained to leap at every beep, if I could just figure out which beep it is.

I grew up in a time of easier-to-identify sounds, when telephones ding-a-linged, cash registers ka-chinged and typewriters clacked; when school bells clanged, fire alarms rang and ambulance sirens wailed. Now they're all being replaced by the *beep-beeps* and *bing-bings* that are the frantic soundtrack of the 21st century.

Many of these high-pitched sounds are strangely hard to locate, even when they're right beside you. I usually fumble around for my cellphone when it rings, because I can't figure out which pants pocket it's in, or even which pants? Maybe it's lost under the armchair again? Several times a week, a mystery beeping goes off somewhere in our house and I run around like a lunatic trying to find whatever it is.

I listen to our bookshelves, to our laundry piles and even inside the fridge. But the beeping always stops before I crack the mystery.

I am bombarded from every side by other urgent electronic sounds. My car beeps constantly, nagging me to put on my seat belt, or turn off the lights, or lock the trunk, or whatever else it's trying to tell me. My printer emits identical beeps when it's out of paper, or ink, or when something is jammed—but which is it? My microwave beeps all the time, just for fun.

Out in the world, elevators and ATM machines beep constantly. TV shows beep when they bleep out swear words. Store machines beep when they swipe your groceries, or when you try to swipe theirs without paying. Then there are security beeps: the loud BEEEEP ... BEEEEP ... BEEEEP that says I'm about to be run down by a Montreal city street cleaner that's backing up; the shrill *beep-beep-beep-beep* that says you have 15 seconds to punch in your house alarm code or an old-fashioned siren will go off alerting a security firm that you are an intruder in your own home.

There are the simple but dreaded beeps of an airline security guard's wand warning you it's time to start your striptease act. Who would have guessed the sound of the 21st century would be the cry of the cartoon Road Runner, the fast-running bird that was always pursued by Wile E. Coyote, crying *"beep-beep"* as it ran? Today we are all Road Runners, frantically beeping as we run for our lives, chased by our own high-speed machines and lifestyles.

Beep-beep! Fasten your seat belt. *Beep-beep!* You have another new email! *Beep. Beep.* Hello, we value your call, but we can't be bothered to take it now, so please don't speak until the beep.

Electronic sounds have become so widespread, ornithologists report many birds are now mimicking our beeps, buzzes, and chirps as part of their mating songs. There are parrots that sound like cellphones, mockingbirds that mimic microwaves and white-bellied caiques that do perfect car alarms.

Will the entire animal kingdom eventually chirp and roar electronically? Or will a future generation of humans switch to more natural sounds, such as a phone ring that sounds like birdsong—instead of vice-versa? Or an alarm clock that sounds like a rooster? Or a cash register that once again makes a soothing *ka-ching*?

Perhaps we will have truly personal ring tones made by gentle New Age machine voices that whisper: *"Suu-ssan ... Suu-ssan.* This is your phone ringing. *Suu-ssan.* I'm in your brown purse, under your makeup and your dirty gym socks. Will you take the call ... or should I?"

Even life itself is now measured in beeps. Hospitals are full of machines whose occasional beeps indicate you are still alive. "I beep, therefore I am." Or not. We are born into the world in a noisy jungle of beeping medical monitors and machines—and we will probably leave the same way.

To beep or not to beep? That is the question future generations must face. But for now, I've got to run. That mystery beeping just started again and I've just figured out what it is. My computer batt-

Biking.com

I was on a bike trip recently with four other guys, cycling several days in the hills of Vermont. But every time we got to a long hill, one guy charged up ahead at breakneck speed, desperate to reach the top a minute before the others. What was he so eager to experience—a breathtaking view? A chance to meditate alone?

No, just a few extra moments to scroll through his Blackberry, check his last 187 emails and fire back some terse three-word answers with his thumbs—before we caught up to him. His cellphone-clutching figure was a routine sight for three days, silhouetted against every hilltop vista and field of wildflowers.

We laughed at our buddy, but we weren't much better. We'd all brought our own smartphones, but none of us had a U.S. Internet plan, so we kept borrowing his to pick up our emails, or confirm our next inn, or check the hour-by-hour forecast.

This was only the start of our technological addiction. Most of us brought our computers which we mainlined each morning on our tiny inn's Wifi. Three guys had GPSs that gave directions while we cycled, to compare with our maps—so we debated our way at every turn.

Guy 1: The map says to turn right at Old Fort Road. This must be it coming up.

Guy 2: No way! According to my GPS, the Old Fort turnoff is 1,537 meters ahead—after the third lane, the second barn, the 17th cow and the 4th rooster.

Guy 3: Nope—it's the third rooster—my GPS shows one rooster just died.

I started the trip smirking at all the "boy-toys" but ended up addicted too. When it rained one afternoon and we were wet and hungry in the middle of nowhere, our GPS generalissimo just pushed the FOOD button on his machine. It instantly flashed the distances to the seven nearest restaurants, pizzerias and grocery stores—with bike route directions for getting there.

It won't be long before GPSs provide onscreen "cyclist take-out" menus, so someone else with a GPS can deliver en route. As you pedal a bike messenger will race up beside you holding a giant Domino box and say:

"Are you the guys who ordered the all-dressed veggie with no onions?"

"No, we wanted the meatball-pepperoni-and-steak combo."

"Okay, the next delivery guy will be by with that in five minutes. My order must be for some other cyclists 857 meters ahead."

Several guys also had "cyclo-computers" that measured precisely how many 1000ths of a meter we went and one kept announcing the exact number of minutes we'd actually been pedaling—versus resting, or eating or debating directions. "We've done 19 km. in 61 minutes and 21 seconds, minus 3 minutes for a juice break, 97 seconds for a bathroom break and 17 seconds for that time I stopped to adjust my helmet." At night he'd calculate the calories we'd burned versus the dinner we'd earned—though no matter how much we cycled, dinner always won.

I didn't realize how weirdly wired we were until me met six mothers one night at our inn who were doing a similar trip in very different style. For starters they had a golden rule: no technology allowed: no GPSs, no computers, no cell phones. Most of them owned these gadgets but had left them back home because they didn't want to be reached by the outside world—or by husbands and kids asking if they should add fabric softener to the dishwasher.

Then how did the women keep tabs on the weather and nearby lunch spots, we asked? It turned out they didn't—because they were super-organized. They never needed emergency "FOOD" because two women were in charge of making appetizers, sandwiches, drinks and brownies. They didn't have debates over directions because another woman was in charge of maps and their one team-sanctioned GPS—and no one argued.

Another woman was designated as team mechanic to deal with bike problems, and we could have used her. When one of our guys bent his chain, we phoned for help to the nearest bike shop, over 70 kilometers away—and lost half a day.

What was the difference between the guys and the girls? About 100,000 years of evolution. The women were the distant inheritants of ancient female "gatherers" who'd once collected and prepared food, as well as kept the campsite in order—while the men were off hunting. Meanwhile we guys were the remnants of those ancient hunters, but with no real weapons or skills. We'd been reduced to firing off emails, tracking our way by GPS and cornering our prey at the nearest roadside pizzeria. We'd become hunters of restaurants, hourly weather forecasts and the exact number of kilometers pedaled—while the women were gatherers of modern ingredients, like sliced prosciutto and jarred Dijon honey-mustard.

At nine p.m., the women said goodnight so they could wake up at five a.m. to make sandwiches, tune their bikes and map their day's route so nothing could go wrong. We kept drinking until midnight, figuring that if anything did go wrong, we could always phone that woman mechanic for help.

Trans-Parent Generation

I was paying at the grocer recently and slipped my bank card into the machine to punch in my PIN number. The owner immediately stood up and turned away to gaze into the distance.

I see this behavior wherever I'm shopping, as clerks and shoppers try to avoid seeing our secret passwords. It's a quaint way we still guard each other's privacy, but it may be the last way—as we enter a transparent new "World with No Secrets."

Each day we are filmed by hundreds of bank-cams, store-cams, street-cams, police-cams and citizen-cams that record our every movement. Every month brings new videos of some politician caught cheating on his spouse, or cheating on his mistress. WikiLeaks has released over a million emails exposing every diplomat's most undiplomatic emails.

Many people also voluntarily share their private lives online with armies of "friends." It's become normal to post your beach photos, even nude photos—while tweeting where you're having a milk shake and who you're sipping it with. All this transparency unnerves many from the older parent generation who view privacy as a sacred right. But many from the younger more transparent generation think privacy is an outdated concept that just gets in the way of publicity. Here's how the two groups think:

GENERATION TRANSPARENT is made up of young people who've lived their whole lives on stage, ever since their embryo was photographed by a womb-cam at eight weeks old. They love to share their experiences with the whole planet on My Face, or Space Book, or Whatever.

My family recently returned from a beach holiday and minutes after we'd stepped through our door my Generation Transparent son had posted his pictures of our family—in our bathing suits—online for the world to see. But when his Generation Parent mother found out she took them down faster than a Chinese government censor.

Generation Transparent loves publicity and spends its days on sites tweeting their friends about what they're doing as they do it.

"Hi. I'm at Metro buying tofu (see attached pic). Where r u?"

"Cool! Buying ygrt rght dwn aisle frm u—I'm in the pic u jst took."

"Oh yeah! Cool—Wave, wave. Kiss, Kiss. ☺ OK, bye fr now. Lts tweet agn at cash. ☺ "

GENERATION PARENT sees all this transparency as a nightmare. They're from a private generation who grew up in the wake of McCarthyism, Nixon wire-tappers and CIA/RCMP spies—and they're paranoid about spreading any bit of personal information about themselves or their families.

Some are still frightened to bank online, or buy a book on Amazon. They'd never share their credit card number online, let alone their personal diary or photos. To them our camera-crazed culture is right out of George Orwell's Big Brother. But to Generation Transparent, Big Brother is just a cool reality show.

From Generation Parent's perspective, the Transparent Generation is naive—they're exposing themselves with embarrassing information that could eventually cost them a job, or an identity theft. The older generation thinks the younger one confuses virtual friends with real ones

But from Generation Transparent's perspective, it's the older generation that's naive and uptight. For many young people public embarrassment and fame often come together, à la Paris Hilton—and that's exactly what they want. They figure the worst that can happen is that someone will show an embarrassing photo of you ten years down the line. The important thing is to make sure you look great in that photo—because it's one more chance to get an audience. And is life really happening if no one is watching?

Generation Transparent can hardly wait for the next stage in our ever more public lives. Perhaps it will be Google Home View where we will all watch each other watching TV. Or Google Anatomy, where you'll check out your friends' X-rays, MRI scans and colonoscopies. Or G-Ogle to let you take a more private peek at your favorite friends, which is already happening on many sexting sites.

Generation Parent may eventually prove right and young people will become more private over time, once they're job-hunting, or spouse-hunting. But it's more likely that privacy will just become a forgotten term—a relic of the 20th century before public and private life blurred. And before Canada's Privacy Commissioner was replaced by a Publicity Commissioner.

I Beg to Agree

ATTENTION, READERS! Before continuing with this story you must agree to all terms and conditions of the author, whether you have read them, or not. (See appendix 17, b-53) This is binding on your heirs and successors. Now say: "*I AGREE!*" If you do not agree, you must leave this page immediately. Thank you for agreeing. We value your acquiescence.

Every time I go online I get offered another legal agreement I can't refuse. Every electronic gadget I purchase requires me to accept endless "terms and conditions" that I automatically become bound to just by using the product.

Like most people I have now agreed to more legal contracts than the World Bank. Yet I have no clue what most of them say. That's because every contract has been worked on by 57 lawyers, hired to make sure each "heretofore" and "whereupon" protects their side. And my only right is to say: "*I AGREE.*"

Every plane ticket I buy guarantees the airline the right to "cancel, terminate, divert, postpone or delay" my flight, with no liability, except an unlikely refund—if I fight them for a year. Every two-year cellphone contract we Canadians sign, but don't read, advises us our carrier may change the contract at any time, including the fees. But we consumers can't break the contract before it's over without paying a hefty penalty—even if they've changed the contract, or the terms of service, or the price, or anything else they feel like changing.

The key to most of these contracts is that companies know we won't read them, because we want their service. Sure, I could read the 35-page legal document that comes with each bank card, credit card, cellphone plan and website I log onto. Then I could write back and dispute clause 17 sub-section 40(f). But what's the point? If I don't agree, my only right is to withdraw from the 21st century. There's never a choice that says: "Let discuss it,"

Just using Google means "you consent to be bound by" a sea of legal clauses their army of lawyers has written. But why find the energy to read them when one of these clauses says: "Google shall have the right to modify the terms of this Agreement at any time, effective immediately upon posting. Accordingly, we suggest that you check this page periodically."

Sure —I'll just read Google's "Terms of Service" web page at breakfast every morning to see if our relationship has changed.

ATTENTION, READERS: The Terms of Service for the story you are reading have recently been updated. When reading it you may not copy, clip, crumple, crease, tear, scribble, stain or otherwise deface this page—or else the author owns your house. If any information in this text is faulty, it is solely the fault of the reader, not the author... If you are offended by something in this text, you agree not to write a letter to the editor, or the author—but nice letters are fine.

What if we all demanded legal contracts in day-to-day life? Before anyone stepped into our house we'd require they sign a 3,000-word waiver absolving us of all injuries, coffee stains or boring dinner table conversations. In fact, before we even started a conversation we'd have them sign a "conversation-rights" clause which ensured that any words we exchanged during dinner were exclusively the right of the "hosting party" not the "conversant"—and guaranteeing us full credit for any use in future conversations.

Everyone would probably sign. The bottom line is that most of us agree to many wordy contracts assuming they are harmless and fair. But every now and then we discover they aren't. Recently I paid $10 to watch a Roger Federer tennis match online on the U.S. Open's official site, where an ad promised I could "sign up and watch now— on your personal computer."

I agreed to their terms of agreement with a fast button click but the site neglected to mention that the picture would be the size of a postage stamp and the tennis ball too tiny to see. It was only afterwards that I checked the "contract" and learned that if anything was wrong with the transmission, the U.S Open was "not responsible" (Translation: no refund).

It's obviously time we consumers had some Terms of Satisfaction to balance all the Terms of Service. It's time we were guaranteed as many legal phrases as big corporations get, in clear language we can understand. In fact it's time we consumers mobilized and organized! It's time we resis –*We are sorry. The story usage agreement for this text has just been updated—and the end of this story is no longer guaranteed to accompany the beginning. Should you feel this is unsatisfactory please check our website, if you can find it somewhere. If you still feel this is unfair, the author wishes you to know the following: "I AGREE."*

Pocket Technology

Like many guys I travel around with an old-fashioned device that's a cross between a filing cabinet, a tool chest and a garbage can.

It's my pants pocket, which contains everything I could possibly ever need: penknife, reading glasses, raffle tickets, Rolaids, newspaper clippings, mini-flashlight, leaky pens, bank stubs, dry-cleaner receipts and enough change to start a video arcade. It's my own personal black hole, where an infinite amount of matter can exist in a very tiny space.

Men make fun of women for what they carry in their purses, but no one knows what we guys carry in our pockets, including us. I never know what will come out next—I reach in for a Kleenex and pull out the passport I lost six months ago.

The male pants pocket was invented in the late 1700s, when tailors got the idea of sewing a change purse right into your pants. It's been a great success for two hundred years, but many men face a growing crisis as modern life outpaces their pockets. More and more guys now have pockets overflowing with gadgets: cameras, phones, GPSs, portable computer keyboards and whatever other new devices men urgently need to carry.

"Look—I just got a combination fishing-rod-pool-cue-barbecue-starter that slips right into your front pocket."

I don't own a personal organizer but I do carry my own personal dis-organizer: a swollen, messy wallet that's close to bursting with today's necessities. It contains countless bank cards, health cards and air-mile cards, wads of bookstore and souvlaki joint loyalty cards and a thousand vital scraps of paper that I keep meaning to sort out.

But sometimes my wallet gets too swollen for my back pocket, which can be embarrassing. I was at the supermarket cash recently, where I couldn't get my wallet out of my pocket no matter how much I wriggled and pulled. Eventually a nice older women behind me volunteered to extricate it, in a long surgical procedure that left many nearby shoppers rolling in the aisles.

The other problem with my pockets is finding things in them, since they don't come with pull-out drawers. I've lost my car key in my pocket so I now carry it on a large ring of useless keys—just so I can find it. When I pull it out, people think I'm a building superintendent.

Then there's my cellphone, a big clunky model that's easy to locate from the bulge in my pockets. But I still miss many of my calls trying to get it out when it rings, while five nearby guys with the same ringtone thrash madly through their pockets too.

While my pockets contain a galaxy of amazing debris, there's one thing they just won't retain—loose change—although that was the reason the pocket was first invented. Every time I sit down I leave a trail of coins on the couch, or under the car seat. Every time I go to a movie, I hear the price of the film clinking onto the floor, as I suffer male fall-out problems.

Sometimes I wonder if there's something wrong with my sitting technique. Did my dad forget to teach me an important lesson? Or was I supposed to read a *Pants User's Manual*: "To sit correctly in pants, place buttocks on chair and clamp knees tightly together to contain loose change. DO NOT CROSS LEGS!"

I'm too old for those cargo pants with knee pockets that make you look like a handyman and too vain for those multi-pocket vests that turn you into a fisherman—but I'm hoping they'll soon invent a pocket that's right for me. I suspect the pants of the future will have a hundred hidden pockets that retain your coins, electronically eject your wallet and have pull-out pouches for sunglasses, cell phones, flashlights, key rings and the latest portable-printer-camera-barbecue-starter.

In fact, just the other day, I clipped out a magazine ad for some khaki pants that claimed to have solved the modern pocket crisis. Unfortunately, I put it in my pocket—and I haven't seen it since.

2

The Health Scare System

The 400 Horsemen of the Apocalypse

Warning: this story will not end if the world ends first.

We're doomed! Do-o-oooomed! Everywhere I turn I'm hearing about the End of the World—again. The apocalypse is coming soon, to a planet near you.

The latest panic was caused by a supposed Mayan prophecy suggesting the world will end on Dec. 21, 2012, at 11:11 a.m.—just in time to ruin our last Christmas shopping season. Apparently the ancient Mayans' 5,000-year calendar stops abruptly that day, so many people fear this must mean the End of Time for all time.

But frankly, I don't have time to worry about it. Mayan Armageddon is just the latest catastrophe-of-the-month to threaten me in a world of constantly-multiplying panics—over everything from from West Nile virus, Asian bird flu and Mad Cow disease to global warming, terrorist shoe-bombers, trans-fat-loaded cereals and genetically-modified mouthwash.

Winston Churchill said there was nothing to fear but fear itself, but nowadays that's way too much. The Institute for the Creation of Panic in Everyday Life is up around the clock figuring out what to scare us to death with next. There's a steady stream of news reports predicting catastrophe by meteor showers, solar flares, tsunamis, gamma ray bursts, a new ice age and a head-on collision with a planet called Nibiru.

There's so much fear out there NASA recently had to calm Americans by announcing the world is not ending any time soon—despite news reports that their Large Hadron Collider could create a black hole that swallows Earth. The Four Horsemen of the Apocalypse have been replaced by 400.

With so many imminent threats it's hard to concentrate on writing this story. What if I'm interrupted by an asteroid, or a tidal wave that literally kills my deadline? There are portents of The End everywhere, if you just pay close attention to them. Last week I opened a box of eggs and four were rotten—what are the chances of that? This week the batteries in my flashlight, my phone and my watch all died mysteriously in the same two days, along with my car battery. So did my toaster, which doesn't even have a battery. Coincidence? Not likely.

Yesterday, I tried to sign in to my online bank account but my keyboard stuck on the letter F and typed it six times. FFFFFF. According to the Nostradamus Code, F is the sixth letter of the alphabet so it actually spelled 666666—the bank PIN number of The Beast. *How much more evidence do you need?*

The truth is that human beings always had plenty to be scared of, from starvation to major diseases like TB, polio and smallpox. But in recent years we've conquered so many real threats we don't have many left to worry about. Instead we have lots of time available to find small threats to worry about—like cellphone rays, sick car syndrome and possible flu shot side effects.

As well, we feel guilty for our comfortable lifestyle—it can't go on, can it? We deserve punishment. That's why we secretly crave some fear and chaos to give urgency to our lives. That's why so many people want ... Apocalypse Now!

Part of me can see the appeal of the apocalypse. It makes me feel important to think the end of time may be coming in my own lifetime. I can tell my grandkids: "I was there when the world ended." It raises the stakes of our mundane modern lives. So maybe we should look at the bright side of Armageddon.

There are some advantages to living in a post-apocalyptic world. For instance, there will be no rush hour traffic anywhere and it'll be easy to find parking spots downtown. Real estate will be cheap, especially on the new Arctic Riviera. There will be no more annoying cellphones chirping in restaurants because there won't be any cellphones, or restaurants. There will be no need to change your snow tires because it will be winter all year round.

You won't even have to turn back the clocks anymore—because it will always be dark, apart from occasional solar flares. So embrace

Armageddon now—or at least plan ahead. Consider taking a big bank loan with a payback date of Dec. 22, 2012.

But beware: there is one thing that could suddenly save us from Mayan catastrophe fear—another looming disaster to fill our brain with new anxieties and let us forget our old ones. Studies show our brains have limited emotional space reserved for fear—usually about seven major worries at once—so panicking about one scary thing often requires us to forget another one.

We've survived and almost forgotten scares over Lyme disease, Ebola, SARS, anthrax and the last big flu fright. So the Mayan catastrophe will likely go the same way, once we get something new to worry about. Fortunately over at the World Institute for The Creation of Panic in Everyday Life they are busy dreaming up new fears as quickly as we get used to old ones. I can practically hear two guys in white lab coats talking:

"OK, Henshaw, we've run through mad cow, swine flu, polluted salmon, and avian flu—even that Mayan panic should be winding down by early 2013—though it *has* been good for us. But what have we got planned for next year?"

"Well, sir, our fear production unit has several possibilities in development—including savage sparrow syndrome, rabid goldfish attacks and anthrax-infected ants. Or we could just announce a standard winter scare campaign about Humidifers That Kill."

"Hmmm. Nothing more interesting?"

"Possibly, sir. There is one thing in the development stage—an Internet virus that jumps from computers to human beings. And *if* it happens, it *could* kill millions of people. Maybe even billions."

"My god, Henshaw, that's fantastic! It doesn't actually exist, does it?"

"Not yet sir, but you know our motto: There is nothing to fear, but the next fear. I'll send out the press kit tomorrow."

My Groan Muscle

This week I discovered an important new muscle that's worked for my body for five decades, though we'd never actually met before. It's my groin muscle, otherwise known as my groan muscle, because that's what it's made me do all week.

I'd never known I owned this muscle until I injured it. Now I know its exact location in my upper thigh, where its sole function is to prevent me from walking. Ever since my injury I scuttle about my house like a crab, trying to walk without moving my legs.

My groin is only the latest in a long list of muscles and other concealed body parts that have been slowly introducing themselves to me since my mid-40s. They have names like the hamstring muscle, the Achilles tendon, the lumbar disc, the sciatic nerve, runner's knee and remote-control elbow. They're giving me an exciting late-life biology lesson I could happily live without.

My injuries are partly because I'm an aging jock who loves sports that no longer love me. In recent years I've been knocked out of action with tennis elbow, basketball ankle, bicycle back and ski knee.

I've wrecked my rotator cuff throwing a football and gone through surgery to mend my meniscus, a tiny "shock absorber" inside my knee whose 50-year warranty suddenly expired during a tennis game. But I keep coming back for more pain, because my mind barely feels middle-aged, though my body claims otherwise.

I'm typical of many guys I know. At my weekly tennis game, my partners are falling like soldiers in battle, felled by ripped tendons, crumbling cartilage and bad backs. You can tell we are an "over 50" league because we've had over 50 injuries this year.

Like all aging athletes, we stand out by our equipment. Young athletes wear football pads, jockstraps and helmets, but aging athletes strap on ankle braces, knee stabilizers and thigh supporters —then go shopping for a groin brace.

The young are focused on winter training, we worry about winter spraining. To prevent injuries, we do endless warm-up exercises before exercising, which sometimes cause more injuries. Afterward, we swallow handfuls of Advil like candy and apply enough ice to our injuries to stock a convention center bar. We spend more time with our physiotherapists than our families.

Recently my own physiotherapist advised me to ease up on strenuous sports. But it's hard to predict what's strenuous any more. My groin injury happened while I was carrying a crate of soda water up our two flights of stairs—when my left leg suddenly went on a work stoppage and announced:

"This is your Perrier-carrying muscle speaking. BE ADVISED: This is the last time I am carrying twelve bottles up those stairs. Next time, buy a two-pack—or drink tap water!"

What activity will prove strenuous next? Will I have to drop other risky sports like wheeling my luggage through the airport, or carrying the newspaper recycling box downstairs, or flipping large omelettes? I'm not complaining, mind you—I know it's all small stuff. I still haven't met the really important parts of my body—like my heart valves, arteries, prostate, liver or kidneys—which all remain complete strangers. But I am starting to wonder if exercise is all it's cracked up to be.

In the race to live forever, many miracle cures are failing—from vitamin pills to endless fad diets shown to have little long-term effect. Exercise is the one thing everyone still agrees is great for you—but will it stand up to long-term research? Perhaps future studies will find that each human only has a certain number of steps in them and that we use them up twice as fast when running?

Until then like many aging athletes, I'll keep on pushing as long as my muscles are willing, but I'll keep lots of frozen peas ready for the days when they aren't. I know that exercise is good for me in the long term—even if it's killing me in the short term.

Junk Memory

I used to be an idiot-savant when it came to remembering phone numbers—but lately I've been losing the "savant" part. I reach into my vast mental Rolodex to call my local pizza joint and end up talking to my dentist. I find myself forgetting other small things too: names, faces, phone codes—and geez, where did I park the car?

I'd like to believe it's not just aging. We live in an era of information overload, with endless stuff to remember—from PIN numbers and alarm codes to the personal security password for my cappuccino-maker. No wonder I sometimes forget my missing glasses are on my head. But age adds to the mental challenge when you suddenly find yourself searching for a simple word.

"Hey honey! Have you seen the uh ... the thing? You know—the one we use to slice cheese?"

"Ohh, you mean the cheese-slicer, Henry."

"That's it! But I'm John, honey. Henry is our son."

I do still have an excellent memory for lots of stuff I'd love to forget. I remember my license plate number when I was eighteen, though I can't remember my current one. I remember that 1066 was the Battle of Hastings—but I can't recall exactly what happened there.

I remember endless scraps of grade school poems, dumb songs and rhyming commercial lyrics that keep playing in my head like alien radio signals. *You'll wonder where the yellow went, when you brush your teeth with Pepsodent.* But I forget what day to take out the garbage. In a world of junk food and junk bonds, I have a junk memory.

Someday when science is ready I want a brain tune-up. I'd be happy to lose any memory of where I was when JFK was shot, or during the moon landing. I'd rather remember all my secret passwords and my passport number and where my car is parked *right now.*

Still, if I can lose my memory, maybe I can find it? There are all kinds of things I'm told I can do to improve my memory—like change my diet. For instance, a recent experiment found that beagles who ate broccoli and Brussels sprouts mixed into their meals had their memories significantly improved. I've tried broccoli and sprouts and it made no difference— maybe I'll try dog food.

Perhaps I could just use acronyms, where you give initials to each item in a list. That way you can easily remember a long grocery list like bread, juice, lettuce, tomato, milk, yogurt, bacon, raisins and fudge—by simply recalling the word BJLTMYBRF.

Also, as my own baby-boom generation ages, I suspect we will invent other solutions, such as mental fitness classes to prevent brain sprains. "Good morning, class. In this first exercise, you'll start by repeating your address three times, then *stre-e-e-tch* your minds to repeat your bicycle combination lock ... then re-e-aally stretch to recall your VISA number and your washer-dryer security access code."

As usual, we boomers can count on one source: the big drug companies. Eventually they will invent incredibly expensive memory drugs that are so powerful we will always be able to find the pill bottles they come in. They will call these drugs "Mental Viagra" and the ads will show an older woman skipping gaily out of a house holding a big green box and shouting: "I remembered—today was recycling day!"

Brain surgeons may also do mental "delete-and-reboot surgery" that erases old junk memories from our brain's hard disk and frees up space for new memories. Or they may invent a block-new-memory drug, so we can save our mental capacity for the times we really need it. In one Sherlock Holmes novel, the Great Detective refuses to listen to his pal Dr. Watson discuss the solar system, because he doesn't want to clutter up his brain with such trivial information.

Holmes doesn't even know the Earth goes round the sun—instead he saves his valuable mental space for useful information that can help him solve his cases. So maybe that's what I'm doing, too. My mental powers are being reserved for high-priority information—like all the Christmas hymns I still know verbatim from my Protestant high school—very handy for a Jewish guy like me.

Sometimes I suddenly find myself crooning "Away in a Manger," or "Onward Christian Soldiers," or entire verses like: "O come let us adore him, O come let us adore him, O come let us ado-o-ore hi-i-m, Chri-i-ist The Lord!"

See—like Sherlock I can remember the important things. Now excuse me while I go out and buy some BJLTMYBRF.

How to Get Fidgetly Fit

I've always been a big fidgeter. Some people can sit through a six-hour meeting and remain as motionless as their chair—but put me there and I squirm like a lobster in a trap. In restaurants I fiddle with the cutlery. At my desk, I tap my toes, jiggle my knees and twirl what little hair I have left.

When there's nothing else to fiddle with, I fidget with my digits. If I were a chameleon I wouldn't last two minutes before a hawk spotted me yawning—or scratching my neck.

All this is to say I was thrilled to see a new study recently that shows I'm not just fidgeting my life away. I'm actually exercising—because fidgeting fights flab. In a large international study by several universities, scientists found that restless fidgety mice are much thinner than those that sit around calmly—though the report didn't mention exactly how mice fidget. Do they twirl their whiskers, bite their nails, or play with their jewelry?

The fact is many of us spend our lives sitting inertly at our desks, TVs and computers when we're not sitting in the car. We are sitting ducks, so to speak, waiting for a *crise de coeur*. But the good news is that every small movement we make counts as a bit of calorie-burning exercise—from tapping our toes (9 calories) to chewing gum (14 calories) to bending over to pick up a pencil (depends how heavy the pencil is). Even people who keep getting up to nibble from the fridge get some exercise, though that's obviously a losing equation.

Mayo Clinic studies show we fidgeters burn an extra 350 more calories a day than you non-fidgeters. That's about the same as a 40-minute daily aerobic workout—which translates into a weight loss of over 20 pounds a year. So it turns out I'm "fidgetly" fit—though it's not really something I'd planned.

Part of my success is that I'm somewhat messy and I get exercise because I'm always poking around in my piles of paper. When I'm desperate to find something I can get quite athletic. "Ohmigod! I have to leave for the airport in ten minutes—where's my passport? I just had it—ohmigod!—it must be under this book! ... No! —maybe under that pile? No!!—Maybe that stack of paper!"

By the time I find it, I've had a major workout.

Now that we know fidgeting is good for you, we should encourage it. Instead of going to finishing school, kids should go to fidgeting school. In our era of childhood obesity, students should be punished for keeping their hands folded neatly on their desks and urged to doodle, wriggle or at least shuffle their feet.

"Jeffrey! Stop sitting still right NOW!—and start squirming!"

Eventually fidgeting will become a hot new health craze. There will be best-selling tapes like "Fidget Your Fat Away" and "Don't Just Sit There Doing Nothing—Fidget!" Jogging will be replaced by Extreme Foot-Tapping and pilates replaced by Aerobic Doodling. Apple will bring out a new app called Fidgetwidget which has no function but to make you fidget with it. Personal fidgeting trainers will fill gyms showing us how to get a total workout with no equipment but our office desk. Say goodbye to the Stairmaster and hello to the Chairmaster, as your boot camp trainer puts you through your exercise drill, barking: "Slouch! Sit up! Slouch! Sit up! .... Terrific! Now gimme a hundred pencil pickups!"

So get with the program and start fidgeting *now* with the new "Freed Fidgetical Fitness Guide"—with tips from a lifetime expert. For instance:

When sitting, cross and uncross your legs repeatedly. Chew on your finger. Scratch when there's no itch. At office meetings, twiddle your thumbs, twirl your hair, twist your ring, floss your teeth or just drum on the desk and play air guitar. You'll drive your colleagues nuts but who cares—let them get fat.

Okay, everyone—now stand up and give me a hundred yawns! And don't forget to wiggle while you work.

Disinformation Overload

This column contains 775 words, 56 sentences, 96 nouns, 83 verbs and between 5% and 65% of your recommended daily humor intake, depending on your sense of humor—and whether you share mine.

I was in the supermarket with my pal Nutrition Guy recently, buying cereal, when he grabbed the box from my hands and studied the ingredients as closely as a legal contract.

"You can't buy this!" he announced. "It's got 16 grams of sugar, 800 milligrams of salt and zero protein. Why don't you just buy a box of salt and sugar for breakfast?"

He wheeled around and scanned a dozen others labels like a nutrition detective. "Here—try this!," he said, handing me an identical brand with "honey clusters." It had a quarter the salt and sugar but ended up tasting the same. I felt like an ingredient-challenged child who shouldn't be allowed to shop alone.

The truth is I've never been an educated eater. I've had bouts of food fear over the years during the Trans Fat Terror Era and the Eggs Are Bad For You Regime (before eggs were good for you again). I've ingested so much olive oil that if they ever discover it's bad for you, I will call Paperman's Funeral Parlor to make an immediate reservation.

But somehow I've managed to stay oblivious to ingredient labels until my recent experience with Nutrition Guy. Ever since, I've been reading them more and enjoying food less. The labels are a bottomless pit of information, disinformation and potential despair. The more I know, the worse I feel.

For instance I've always liked canned soups for lunch in winter but when I read the ingredients they're not really soups—they're salt with soup flavoring. I envision the person who's employed as official Soup-Salter, sitting at the assembly line and adding wheelbarrows of salt to every can while the official Salt-Taster shouts "More! More!"

The other omnipresent ingredient is sugar, disguised as dextrose, fructose, glucose, sucrose and other rhyming words that make you morose. Adding to the confusion, some ingredients are listed in grams and others in milliliters per portion size—though a portion may be 4 potato chips and I eat 400. To me what these labels really say is: "this product contains 39 gms. guilt, 27 mgs. remorse, 5 mls. shame and 2 pangs regret."

Nutrition Guy thinks supermarkets should have in-store ingredient advisers to educate the label-challenged like me. Lately there are guys at my local Provigo wearing chef toques and offering samples. Maybe they could exchange their chef outfits for doctor costumes, then offer consultations.

Good afternoon, sir. Welcome to the salt'n'soup section. I'll be your nutrition adviser today. Do you have any special food concerns?

Yeah. I've got high blood pressure, my cholesterol's high and I think I'm lactose intolerant.

Excellent, sir! I recommend you avoid our chunky soups, creamy soups and tasty soups—and try this broccoli, asparagus and kale soup with omega-enriched seaweed mulch and condensed Brussels sprout paste. It comes in "Astonishingly high sodium," "Extremely high sodium, or our Heart Happy "Simply-excessively high sodium."

New York's Mayor Bloomberg has now made fast food restaurants provide calorie counts on menus and it probably won't be long before ingredient-listed menus are mandatory throughout North America. I agree we should have this information in principle, but I'm not sure I want to know it personally.

Will I enjoy my dessert as much when the *crème brulé* lists two cartons of cream and a half box of sugar? How about that quesadilla bacon burger when it lists "3200 calories and 9 years of my daily recommended nitrates?"

Once restaurants start listing ingredients where next? We live in an increasingly transparent society—so what else should we know? Movies have warning labels like PG 13, but why not go further? "This film contains 57 explosions, 43 stabbings, 19 shootings, 13 decapitations and 567 expletives."

Or: "This shirt was made by Bangledeshi workers living 17 to a hut making $1 an hour. No Silk worms were harmed."

How about government-enforced warnings for government-run lotteries, listing the risk ingredients. "This lottery ticket has .000026 chance of winning up to $50 and .0000000000000000001 of winning any sum containing more than two zeros."

How much information is too much information? If my favorite restaurants ever get menus with ingredients I'd like the option of not reading them. The waiter can say: "Good evening—will you be having your menu today with calories, or without?"

Do I really want to know all of life's ingredients? Is ignorance bliss, or just the road to a coronary?

You have now consumed your recommended portion of words. Stop reading immediately.

You didn't listen. Don't blame me if you go blind.

Studies May Be Bad for Your Health

There's been lots of news lately from The Institute of They Say—the experts who keep telling us what's good and bad for our health.

In a study by the Institute of Something Or Other, they say eating your vegetables doesn't prevent cancer—after years of countless experts telling us it does. They also say that exercise doesn't cause us to lose much weight, like we thought it did when we were jogging 5000 kilometers because *they* said we should.

Frankly, it's hard to keep up with "they," whoever they are, because they keep changing their minds.

For years they said chocolate was fattening and bad for you, but lately it's become great for your health, according to the University of I'm Not Quite Sure Where. They say that one small square of dark chocolate a day can decrease your risk of heart problems by nearly 40 per cent. It won't be long before someone declares chocolate a drug and packages it as Super Vitamin CH—to be administered with Vitamin Ice Cream and Vitamin Fudge. However, before you start pouring chocolate syrup on your cereal, they also say that eating large amounts of chocolate can lead to weight gain, which can increase your risk of heart problems.

So maybe you should switch to coffee instead—it's practically a health food according to recent studies from the University of More and More Studies. They say that caffeine may help prevent Parkinson's, gallstones, colon cancer and memory loss—and it may even reduce drowsiness.

But according to the Institute of Equal and Opposite Studies, caffeine can also cause nausea and high blood pressure in mice who've ingested 30 cups of double espresso a day since birth.

Part of the problem with studies is that we are a studious society. No sooner does one research team announce that something is good for you than 147 other health researchers apply for grants to do more studies—and the next thing you know it's bad for you, or at least way more complicated than you thought.

That's why my own philosophy is to enjoy what you can while they say it's good for you—because you never know when they will suddenly declare it's bad for you. For instance, I enjoyed many happy years on the red wine diet when they said moderate drinking was healthy.

But after 3,593 more studies by the Institute of There's No Way Drinking is Healthy, they now say wine isn't that good for you. There's also a heated trans-Atlantic debate between laid-back European wine researchers who define moderate drinking as three drinks a day—and sober North American ones who define moderate as half a drink to one.

So it all depends where you do your drinking—and sadly I do mine in North America, so I have to cut back.

I'm also back to eating eggs after many years when they were scorned as the cigarettes of the breakfast table—in cartons that should have been labeled "death by cholesterol." Now they say eggs are good for you again, since The Institute to Promote the Egg Industry has funded many studies of their own that show—surprise!—eggs are good in 'moderation', whatever that is.

The latest Great Satan of the food world is salt which has triggered more public safety alerts than airport terrorists. In health-conscious New York City, a salt-shaker in public is now legally classified as a weapon—and pointing it at someone's plate is considered a criminal act, unless you are licensed to salt.

So I'm cutting back on salt until The Institute to Rehabilitate Salt sponsors new studies that show salt is healthy because it makes you thirsty, so you crave more water, which is good for you. I'm also eating loads of vegetables nowadays since they say they're supposed to be excellent for your health. But with so many studies being done on them don't be surprised to see a future headline saying: SALADS MAY CAUSE CANCER.

The truth is that food is way more complex than we think and no individual food is likely to save you or kill you. So enjoy your chocolate, caffeine, salmon, eggs and vegetables while they say you should. But keep an eye open for sudden reversals by new studies.

Lately I read that swimming after lunch is actually very safe, but taking a walk after dinner has some risk. So I've started swimming after dinner.

How to Smoke Your Phone

I was in a movie theater last week when that new cartoon warning came on urging us not to talk or text. Suddenly I remembered those old no-smoking signs they had outside movie theaters decades ago—and I realized the transformation is complete.

The cellphone has become the cigarette.

Everywhere you look, people hold phones instead of cigarettes to their mouths, exhaling words instead of smoke. Meanwhile, the anti-cell lobby is becoming as vociferous as the anti-smoking one. How else does the cellphone resemble the cigarette? Let me count the ways:

- It's an oral habit. Cigarettes were an ideal way for fidgety people to do something with their hands, whether they were rolling, lighting, twirling, tapping or dragging on them. But the cellphone has just as many rituals to keep fidgeters busy.

You can check your messages, organize your mail—then reorganize it—as well as text, Skype, surf, check the weather for the 42nd time, or just fondle the phone in your hand, like a cigarette. Instead of making smoke rings, the cellphone just rings—and while you light up a cigarette, your phone lights up by itself.

- Physically, phones have shrunk from the size of a brick to the size of—a cigarette pack. Men often carry them in their shirt pockets like they do their smokes. Women dump them in their purses like cigarettes and spend just as much time looking for them. But at least you can phone your phone in your purse, while you can't phone your cigarettes.

In restaurants you lay your phone right on the table to have instant access just like you did your cigarette pack when you were still allowed to smoke in restaurants. It can't be long before men start slipping their phones up their T-shirt sleeves, like they did cigarette packs decades ago.

Cells are addictive like cigarettes, too—we clutch them while walking, driving, eating and even talking to other people beside us. I suspect that after sex, many people now reach over to get their messages, instead of getting their smokes.

• Just like Big Tobacco, the Big Phone Industry grows by targeting the young with cheap plans aimed at hooking them for life. A three-pack-a-dayer smoked 60 cigarettes daily. Today's average teenager sends over 100 texts a day—and probably spends as much time texting as most people ever smoked.

• For decades cigarettes were an omnipresent film prop that filled movie screens with swirls of smoke, while film characters smoked as they confessed their intimate secrets to the camera. Today cigarette smoke is largely gone from the screen but cellphones ring constantly behind the scene and are used as props for characters to talk into and confess their intimate secrets.

If Hamlet were written today, his anguished words spoken to Yorick's skull would probably be replaced by a cellphone soliloquy.

• Smoke pollution aggravates us—but cellphones create noise pollution that's just as annoying. Instead of second-hand smoke, you get second-hand conversation. A phone can pollute a room quicker than a cigarette, as in a supermarket line when you hear someone hollering about their cousin's prostate operation. Or planning the night's menu:

"HI HONEY! They're out of salmon steaks, so I'm getting tilapia, OKAY? But we need a side dish—Look in the PANTRY to see if we have potatoes!! What?—Honey—I CAN'T HEAR YOU!"

Meanwhile, in the next aisle a teenager is anxiously saying: "Like I called him like an hour ago, like, but I don't like think he likes me anymore like I like him, like."

• One big difference is that smoking definitely causes cancer while studies are very inconclusive on cellphones. The science isn't there, though the fear is growing fast. Many people wear hands-free sets for protection just like smokers used cigarette filters. But you don't see as many in Montreal as in Toronto, Calgary and Vancouver. Quebecers always liked strong, unfiltered cigarettes like Gitanes— and they don't like to filter their phones either.

- Now that mobile phones are more common than cigarettes, anti-cell advocates are becoming as zealous as anti-smokers. There are no-cell sections in many trains, hotels and restaurants instead of no-cigarette sections. Most flights have banned cells just as they did cigarettes. We will probably live to see cells banned in bars too, so you'll have to phone outside in the snow.

For now we still give babies fake cellphones for their cribs like we used to hand them chocolate cigarettes. But how long can it be before we see class actions against Big Phone companies for deliberately addicting our kids to the nicotine of words, with cheap all-you-can-speak plans? How soon before the first cellphone noise pollution settlement?

Eventually there will be a cigarette app on your phone that lets you flick a video flame and safely inhale a tobacco-flavored scent? At last, you will be able to smoke your cellphone.

3

Urban Chaos Theory

Breaking Up with the Grocer

I'm finally able to walk down the Main, my local shopping street, now that my old grocer has retired and closed his doors. For several years I wouldn't pass his store for fear he'd be standing outside watching me. I'd been a loyal customer for decades, buying my fruit and yakking with him. But the older he got the older his produce became, and then a perky new Indian grocer opened with fresher fruit and a prettier look—and well, to make a long story short, I left my guy for The Other Grocer.

But my old grocer was always outside, sitting under his canopy. For a while we waved like old pals but eventually he started to glare silently and give me *The Look*—and I could almost hear him thinking: "Are you ever coming back ... or have you found someone else?"

I knew I wasn't returning and eventually he knew too, so I started walking on the other side of the street to avoid my "loyalty guilt." It was a relief when he retired recently and I can walk the street freely, without worrying about *The Look*.

I suffered the same "loyalty guilt" when I changed barbers a while back. I'd been with Mario for years but things had gotten strained in recent times. He talked endlessly about his family, his boat and his daughter, the teacher and I'd heard all his stories so many times I was avoiding getting haircuts—and my hair was getting even longer than his stories.

So I quit, and ever since I don't walk down that stretch of street downtown because he's often at the window watching the passing crowds—and I know I couldn't take it if he gave me *The Look*. Things might turn out like they did with my friend who left his Westmount dentist. One day he bumped into him on a nearby street and they exchanged greetings and the dentist gave him *The Look*.

"You know," said the dentist, "I haven't seen you for a long time."

"That's true," murmured my friend, embarrassed.

"It's been a lot more than six months.

"Yeah, that's true. I've ... been real busy. "I'll call you soon."

"Don't bother," replied the dentist smoothly. "I'll have my secretary call you in the morning to make an appointment."

By nature, I'm a loyal customer who sticks with even giant faceless companies for decades. I've had the same bank my whole adult life and I kept my phone company for decades till I found out it was charging me twice what it was offering new customers. I quit and let the phone people know why—and they've been phoning me ever since making sweet promises like a jilted lover. But at least I don't have to run into them on the street and get *The Look.*

When you live in a city long enough the streets are haunted with abandoned relationships. I had a favorite Spanish restaurant for years, where I ate the same dish so regularly I was known as Mr. Omelet.

Eventually I stopped going, but occasionally I'd bump into the waiters and they'd say: "My God—it's been so long! Where have you been, Mr. Omelet? We never see you anymore. Have you given up omelets?"

The truth was I'd found a new Spanish place nearby with a much better omelet, but what could I say? I considered dropping in once for old time's sake but it's like bumping into an old lover. They get nostalgic and say: "It's been great to see you—I'll call you soon."

And you have to admit—yes—I'm seeing another restaurant.

How do you tell them you've fallen in love with an elegant little Asian dish in the neighborhood that's seduced your stomach with its culinary play? How do you inform your long-time Polish chef that his cuisine is too heavy for our lean times—and gives you heartburn? Or confide in your Chinese restaurant guy that "the Hunan dumplings are more silky down the street and they don't over-steam the broccoli."

It's easier to cross the street, or avoid the street entirely. There must be a long German word for the-feeling-of-loyalty-guilt-you-get-when-you-pass-a-place-you-once-loved-but-don't-anymore; the sense that it was good while it lasted but I'm sorry, we just can't see each other again.

Maybe there are people out there who have the same relationship with me—disillusioned readers who don't pass the Montreal *Gazette* building for fear I may wander out and show them my latest column. Or neighbors on my street who avoid passing my house because they've fallen for the young music reviewer just down the *Gazette* page from me.

Don't worry, I forgive you. I am out on my balcony watching— but I won't give you *The Look*. I'm just keeping an eye out for my barber.

Josh vs. Josh

There's a growing turf war on our streets and there's no room for both gangs. One is encased in 3,000 pounds of steel and surrounded by surround sound and seventeen coffee-cup holders. The other gang is perched on 23 pounds of fragile aluminum and protected by six-ounce helmets. It's a battle between bikers and motorists over who will rule the roads.

There's a two-wheel revolution sweeping our city and many others, as biking turns from sport to transport. But motorists are irritated at their shrinking slice of road. That's led to more and more road rage, with cyclists and motorists each giving each other the gears.

I spend summers on my bike and winters in my car—so I have a split personality on wheels. There are two Joshs warring in the bosom of a single driver—Car-Josh and Bike-Josh—with very different mentalities, depending on who's driving.

CAR-JOSH: When I'm in my car, I see bikes as a two-wheeled nuisance, the pigeons of urban wheel-life, flitting about and flouting every rule. Many cyclists sail through red lights and stop signs as cavalierly as politicians in a motorcade. They drive down streets the wrong way, ride on sidewalks and often drive without lights at night, in black ninja clothing and sunglasses while talking on their cellphone. Yet they are surprisingly nimble and hard to hit.

Car-Josh also resents the self-righteousness of many cyclists, who think "four wheels bad, two wheels good"—and dismiss cars as 3,000 pounds of pollution. Yet there are more two-wheeled cranks around all the time, and more bike paths to suit them. Why can't these Spandex-clad Tour de France wannabes just obey the law like cars?, fumes Car-Josh. In fact, why can't they get bumpers, engines and four wheels—and become cars—so I don't have to worry about them. Until that happens, let them eat my exhaust.

BIKE-JOSH sees things differently. This part of me sees my city's streets as the Wild West of motoring, filled with bullying SUVs, kamikaze cabbies and testosterone-drugged teenagers driving 150 kilometers an hour, while typing text messages into their phones to say they'll be five minutes late at Starbucks. And they're all out to kill Bike-Josh. They roar past only centimeters from my ears. They tailgate me, honk me and rarely offer me the right of way, although they're encased in steel armor while I'm just wearing skin.

Guerrilla tactics are my only hope against these gorillas. I cycle down narrow streets the wrong way, because I'd rather see the enemy coming than let it sneak up from behind. I rarely wait for green lights because that gives drivers a head start to gun their engines and squeeze me between their car and the parked cars up ahead.

I'm a scofflaw outlaw who grabs any opening he sees. When I'm cycling home on traffic-clogged rush hour streets, I feel like prey. I have one eye flitting behind me for tailgaters and the other eye scanning ahead in case some moron like Car-Josh suddenly swings open the door of his parked car and turns me into a human cannonball.

My only escape hatches are sidewalks, my unofficial emergency bike paths. They're the one place I feel safe from predators when biking with my twelve-year-old son—though we usually travel on them more slowly than pedestrians. After all, it's their sidewalk not ours.

I know many car-drivers want police to crack down on scofflaw cyclists, instead of scofflaw motorists. They want cyclists to behave like cars, but Bike-Josh feels he is not a car—and if he ever has to stop-and-start at every deserted stop sign—then he may as well switch to a car for good.

Life is getting better for Bike-Josh and his guerilla kin. Cycling paths are spreading everywhere, even if they're just painted lines on a busy street. Motorists are gradually starting to respect them and letting bikers use them without brushing up against our knees. When I'm on them, I feel safer, calmer and ready to be more law-abiding. And if I sometimes look a tad righteous, it's because I'm recycling my own cycle power, while Car-Josh is burning fuel.

Bike-Josh and Car-Josh do have something in common. They both dream of a day when they can share the streets more easily. For that to happen, Car-Josh needs to take a chill pill and give bikes more breathing room, while Bike-Josh has to stop behaving like an outlaw.

But who will take the first step in bringing the two together? Anyone know a good cyclo-therapist?

Who Took the Chit out of Chat?

I took an airport cab recently where the driver and I chatted non-stop the entire ride—only we weren't talking to each other. He was yakking on his cellphone and I was on mine, each of us in our own private worlds.

I love talking to cabbies, armchair experts on everything from local news and traffic to politics in their distant native lands. But more and more of them now pull out their hands-free phone the second I sit down and treat me like a package in the back seat. Ask them a question and they'll say: "Excuse me sir, but I am talking here to my mother in Cairo."

Since they're ignoring me, I ignore them. It's a chance to get some work done—but one less chance to enjoy the company of strangers.

Cabs are just one of many places where random conversations with strangers are getting hard to find. We used to talk to the butcher, baker and candlestick-maker—but most of them have been replaced by big-box stores where customer relations matter more than human relations.

The clerks at Staples, Bureau En Gros and elsewhere always ask: "Did you find everything you were looking for, sir?" But they don't really want you to say anything but "yes I did, thanks"—even if you didn't. Trying to make conversation with them is practically rude. I tried to chat with a supermarket cashier recently and she looked at me like she was going to call for security. "Attention! Attention! Weird bald guy at Aisle 3 cash who wants to TALK."

I can still chit-chat at my local cheese shop, newsstand, or stationery store, but the neighborhood gas guy who checked my oil and talked to me about the weather is long gone. He's been replaced by a self-service place with a cashier who's way too busy selling lottery tickets to converse.

In recent years bank machines have ended our chats with tellers, while the phone operator has long vanished, replaced by PRESS 1 machines. It's the same when we phone offices, where I used to get personal secretaries I'd gradually get to know. But now I get a voice machine instead—or at best the voice mail of a secretary. An hour later they return my call and leave a message and later I call and leave them one—and by the time we're through messaging we've said what we needed and don't end up talking.

This even extends to friends and family. For much of my life I called my pals at home and never knew who'd pick up the phone. I might end up talking to their spouse, or their kids, or their cleaning person—in unexpected chats. But the last couple of years I barely remember my friends' home numbers—I just call their cellphones, which they answer immediately. As a result, I never have random chats with whoever else answers—because no one else does.

The irony is we've never heard more about "chat." There are chat rooms, chat lines and chat shows—but real chat is disappearing. We walk in crowds of people, all talking on our cellphones, living in our own private cells. We listen to iPods, each with our own soundtrack. We send email invitations instead of making phone calls because fewer words are lost in random chatter. But something else is lost as isolation replaces conversation.

Taxis are even more isolating in cities like New York where most cabs now have passenger TVs so you end up watching your own screen in back while the driver chats privately up front. Maybe we should develop robot taxis that are more chatty, to take over this human task.

"Welcome to Robo-Cab. Please state your destination."

"Downtown, please. Place Ville Marie."

"Thank you. Robo-Cab now proceeding to destination. Would you prefer my Silent Driver function or my Chatty Driver one? I can converse on many subjects:

Press 1 to hear me complain about construction hassles on the Champlain Bridge.

Press 2 to discuss politics in my native land—I was built in China.

Press 3 for a rant on cheap taxi fares and how many hours I put in driving."

Until then what can you do to put the chit back in chat? Next time you're at the supermarket, put down your cellphone and talk to your aisle-mate. When you go to the dentist, ask the assistant how *her* teeth are. Or try discussing the news with the guy at your newsstand.

Chat up a stranger today—and help make society more social.

Exit the Eccentrics

I mourned the death of the Great Antonio recently, and I had lots of company. The huge outpouring of nostalgic coverage was about more than the loss of a city legend; it marked the fact that Montreal's great characters are all fading away.

Antonio was a huge strongman who would periodically stop a city bus, wrap a large chain round it, then tug the vehicle down the street with the amazed passengers still inside. But the Great Bus Puller was the last of a dying breed that just isn't being replaced.

When I started reporting in the late-seventies, Montreal was filled with outlandish personalities—like Kid Oblay, a yakky battered ex-boxer known as the Mayor of Ste. Catherine St., and Bang'em-and-Shotgun Ferguson, a retired bank robber who hung out at Ben's deli describing his heists.

On the Main, Schwartz's tiny counter stools sagged under the weight of several 300-pound characters who had names like "Tiny" and "Big Animal." They were loud guys who ordered their smoked meat fat, with *speck*—huge chunks of extra fat that made your heart stop. And eventually theirs.

Now, they've been replaced by regular-sized people who prefer their sandwiches lean.

Only a few years ago we lost the Mayor of the Main, another ageing 300-pounder who wore a battered cowboy hat and chewed a foot-long cigar. His office was a bench on the Main, by Warshaw's Polish supermarket where he sold pens and watches from a paper bag and filled your ear with the days when he chauffeured for Liberace and Jimmy Durante.

But the Mayor was driven from his neighborhood and his "office" by rising rents and died soon after, while other legends have also left the stage. Kid Oblay died a few years ago, along with the Balloon Man, whose giant silhouette so resembled his own balloons, you thought he'd float away.

The Harmonica Lady hasn't been at her old Prince Arthur Street post for years, although I can't say I miss her. She played an agonizingly bad harmonica by the outdoor tables and wouldn't stop until you paid for her to go away and have a beer.

Even madcap activist Bicycle Bob is mellowing since he hit seventy. He used to smear himself in ketchup and lead "die-ins" with cyclists who laid down in rush-hour traffic to protest the "autocracy." Now he writes bike poetry and leaves the antics to younger city characters. But few are left.

There's the Operaman and his singing family on Ste. Catherine Street, a few colorful drag queens on the Lower Main and the strange guy who passes my house each day with a loin cloth skirt and an eight-foot biblical staff. There's also the aging King of Sit-ups, who shows up at charity events to do 45,000 sit-ups. But many of these people are performers, not just characters living out their daily lives.

Where are today's genuine replacements? Have they fled the downtown core for other areas—or the suburbs? Is there a Harmonica Lady and a Balloon Man at a mall somewhere in the suburbs? Have our city characters followed other refugees down the 401 to Toronto?

I suspect they've just run out of space. There's really no room for these types anywhere in our laundered society, where larger-than-life street characters are often dismissed as wackos, or dangerous or bad role models for kids. Today, it's tougher to make a living on the street, like so many of the old guys did. There's an army of young panhandlers out there fighting for the same few bucks, while eccentric street performers now go off to circus schools, or join the Cirque de Soleil.

If the Mayor of the Main were still around today, he'd be forced to open ATM bank doors for people, while Harmonica Lady would never get a city street musician permit. And who would put up with the Great Antonio? I remember seeing him on Ste. Catherine Street in his heyday, with his giant beard and naked chest, as he lumbered up to an idling city bus 50 times his size, then fastened his monster chain to it. The driver and passengers just stared in awe as he towed them away to the cheers of enthralled spectators.

But if a new Antonio ever tried this today, half the passengers would call the cops on their cellphones to say a lunatic had taken them hostage. Minutes later, the anti-terrorist squad would have Antonio surrounded with megaphones and mace. Eventually the social workers would take over and put Antonio on Prozac and a non-cholesterol diet, and he'd eventually wind up giving miracle weight-loss lessons on late-night TV.

We live in a safer, more civilized society, but also more sanitized. A great city needs great characters but how do we develop the next generation? Maybe we should open a training school for city eccentrics? Or offer Canada Council grants to audacious activists and budding bus-pullers?

How about a new TV show called "Eccentric Idol" to unearth all the unknown colorful personalities hiding out in their basements here and across Canada. Let's find the Spoon Man and Harmonica Lady of tomorrow, the next Great Antonio.

Let's vote for a new Mayor of the Main and Ste. Catherine Street Our city still has lots of character, but it sure could use some characters.

Bless My Mess

I have a disorder disorder.

I'm writing this story from an office that's a masterpiece of mess, a mountain range of crumpled paper, yellowing files and old bus passes that swamp my desk and tumble on the floor. But despite the shocked look of visitors, there's method to my messiness.

Like many messy deskers, I know where things are—sort of. One recent British study showed we clutterers actually find stuff faster than you neatniks, because we instinctively know where everything is. Just don't ask to see the study—I'd have to find it in my mess.

Whatever the truth, the times are not on my side. There's a crusade of cleanliness sweeping the continent, a tide of tidiness led by the armies of the neat and their weapons of mess destruction. You see it in the growing industry of electronic organizers, desk organizers, closet organizers and wall organizers cluttering the world.

You see it in endless new books like *Winning the War Between You and Your Desk,* written by "personal organizers" who charge $300 an hour to re-make your mess. There are reality shows with names like *Clean Sweep* that send SWAT teams of neatniks into the lairs of the messy to reform us, offering salvation through sanitation. But you won't see any shows that mess up neat people's offices. The neat are evangelists, but we messy are too embarrassed to preach.

I see this tyranny of the tidy as a growing menace, because my mess is me. If you could see inside my brain, I suspect it would look like my office, a swirl of ideas tumbling off mental shelves and reassembling into new ideas that cover the floor of my imagination. I'm a "piler," not a filer—partly because I don't know what to file things under. I clip loads of newspaper articles, looking for ideas, but can rarely figure out how to categorize them. Besides, when I do file something away, I usually forget it's there—because out of sight is out of mind for me.

Yet as long as an item is somewhere in my piles, I bump into it all the time—and often find a sudden use for it. To neatniks, an organized desk is an organized mind, but for me, an empty desk is an empty mind. After all, there is some method to my chaos. My desk mess works on geological principles: 2012 is piled on top, with 2011 and 2010 somewhere below. I can locate most documents by the number of layers I go down.

Other messy deskers I know work with the "volcano" style system. There's an empty crater around their computer, surrounded by steep volcanic walls of mess that get older and yellower as they rise, until useless debris falls on the floor, like lava. We messy have our own sense of order.

That's why people like me don't want people to mess with our mess, or tell us to clean off our desks. It's like cleaning out our minds—or performing an environmental lobotomy.

I believe a little chaos creates unexpected ideas. If Archimedes had been neater, he wouldn't have let his bathtub overflow and invented his theory of water displacement. If Isaac Newton had worried about getting his pants dirty, he wouldn't have gone to sleep under a tree, then been hit by an apple and discovered gravity.

Thomas Edison was messy. So were Isaac Bashevis Singer, Marilyn Monroe, Winston Churchill and Albert Einstein (whose desk was even messier than mine). So if you're a secret mess who's hidden your office from the world, it's time to come out of the closet and bring your mess with you. You're not really disorganized—you're "organizationally special." And it's time to show some messy pride.

In the meantime, if any of you neatniks are interested, I'm available for consulting. For $300 an hour, I'll happily come and mess up your office. I've started working as a personal dis-organizer.

No Island is an Island

*Complete the following sentence: The Champlain Bridge will
be closed:*
a) From 9 p.m. to 9 a.m. Monday through Friday
b) From 9 a.m. to 9 p.m. Monday through Sunday
*c) From 9 a.m. to 9 p.m. and 9 p.m. to 9 a.m. Monday through
Sunday—and the rest of the time, too.*

If you answered c) you are a Champlain Bridge commuter like
me who's spent hundreds of hours of your life marooned in
bridge construction. That's enough time to learn Mandarin or get a
correspondence degree in astrophysics. Yet despite this, the Champlain
is still a disaster, say reports from two independent engineering
companies. To paraphrase the reports:

> The Champlain Bridge is falling down, falling down, falling
> down,
> And if we don't act very fast, we'll all ... drown.

The reports say "Canada's busiest bridge" is in danger of crumbling,
or partly caving in—and in a mild earthquake it could totally
collapse. If this was Toronto they'd already have called in the army.
But don't get alarmed—because the Federal Department of Crumbling Infrastructure that owns the bridge says it's fine, and just needs
another $150 million in patches. That would mean so many years of
construction they'd rename it *Pont Fermé*.

Whatever happens we commuters obviously need additional
emergency measures starting now. Here are some suggestions:

1. We could all wear safety helmets when crossing the Champlain
as we do when biking, rock-climbing, car racing or driving under
our crumbling overpasses. We should forget seatbelts, which only
cause trouble when trying to escape a car underwater—it's better to

wear life preservers while kids should drive with floaties.

The bridge should also have emergency escape chutes—like airplanes. Maybe the government could install a giant airbag under the bridge that opens in any emergency to catch us—or at least a sturdy fishing net.

2. The Japanese were remarkably calm during their massive earthquake partly because they'd had so many training drills to learn what to do. So why don't we Montrealers have emergency bridge drills? Imagine the scene: We'd arrive at the bridge in rush hour, get stuck in the usual monster traffic jam—and suddenly hear sirens and a loudspeaker announcing: "This … is a bridge drill. Please leave your cars immediately!"

I'm sure that, just like the Japanese, we would all politely evacuate our cars and proceed in orderly fashion to the sides of the bridge. And like the Japanese we'd form neat lineups for our pretend "escape"—waiting patiently during instructions and bowing politely as we let women and children go first. Wouldn't we?

At the very least, all bridge commuters should pass an ice-water swimming proficiency test before being allowed on the bridge—and non-swimmers should be prohibited from using it.

3. Once construction starts on the bridge most traffic will have to be rerouted, but where—since all our other bridges are overcrowded and collapsing too. It's time to think outside-the-bridge. New York has created hundreds of ferries like the Long Island Ferry and the Brooklyn Ferry. Why don't we do the same—with fleets of giant ferryboats that carry tens of thousands of people across the river.

We can supplement this with thousands of freelance boats—yachts, rowboats, dinghies, fishing vessels, rafts and even Windsurfers to get people home at night—in a kind of nightly evacuation of Dunkirk. Let's throw in a Bixi canoe rental service, some hot-air balloons and maybe a zip line for James Bond types. It would make the river very colorful. If we add gondolas with singing rowers, we'd become the Venice of North America.

4. We may need to think even bigger. Face it: the real problem isn't our collapsing bridges—it's the water surrounding Montreal on all sides. Who needs it? I'm sure modern technology has some way to dam the river and drain the St. Lawrence for good. What's so great about being an island anyway, apart from the view?

I suggest "The Miracle Moses Solution." Let's reroute the river water to the back side of the island for surfing competitions—à la Big Sur. Or just sell the river to the U.S., where water is in demand—let them worry about re-routing and moving it. Once the river is drained, we'll rename it St. Lawrence Canyon or St. Lawrence Gulch and cross by jeep, dirt bike or camel rental. Trust me, you won't miss the water at all—so don't cry me a river.

The future of Montreal is unabridged.

Bonjour! Mon nom est Josh

This column was written in French for L'actualité *magazine in spring 2012 and was re-blogged a day after the Quebec election win by the PQ. It became the most widely-read online piece in the magazine's history—and elicited almost a thousand e-mails from francophones, most calling for language reconciliation after a divisive election. The following is a slightly edited English translation.*

Hi, name is Josh—and I confess, I'm a Quebec Anglophone. In fact I'm a typical Montreal anglo—I'm Jewish. Like most Jews I went to the English Protestant School Board of Montreal, because the French Catholic Board didn't want us back then.

So I see myself as a Jewish Protestant. That's because I spent every morning of my childhood learning all these traditional Christian hymns that only Jews in Montreal sing. For instance:

Jesus loves me, this I know, for the Bible tells me so...

and

O Little child of Bethlehem, how still we see thee rise...

I can go into any synagogue full of Montreal Jews, and lead them in a rousing chorus of *Onward Christian Soldiers*, and they'll all know the words—including the rabbi!

Now unfortunately, while I was learning all these Protestant tunes, I didn't learn much French, because English schools didn't really teach that language in Quebec. When I went to school, at Sir Winston Churchill High, I did have a high school French teacher—Mrs. Schwartz. She taught me French twice a week with an English West End accent—that was one part Paris and two parts Cavendish Mall. But it turned out to be incomprehensible once I was old enough to go East of Schwartz's Deli.

I grew up on a street called Deleppy—and I was fifteen before I found out it was actually called De L'Épée. I found this out when I took my first cab home alone and the francophone driver couldn't find my street—even though we kept driving right by the street sign.

Fortunately, in my late teens I moved to downtown Montreal where I finally started to understand how Montreal worked. I lived in an area full of francophones on a street I called Gene Manz. This was obviously a cousin of Rue Jeanne Mance, the name every francophone I met called it. Same went for Pine Avenue which francophones all mysteriously called Avenue Pins.

But slowly I started to adapt and speak French better in this francophone city full of anglophones, allophones and xylophones. I worked in French, I dated in French I even voted for René Lévesque in 1976 to boost French power at a time I thought we needed it. I guess it worked.

My anglo wife and I also sent our son to French school for eight years, where at first he spoke a strange hybrid language—and came home saying thing like "Dad—I want a *collation*" (snack).

Even today he thinks buying milk at the corner *dépanneur* is standard English throughout Canada—just like taking the *Métro*, or the *autoroute*. Our goal was to make sure he spoke French better than me and we succeeded. At age sixteen he's bilingual and totally embarrassed to hear my pre-historic anglo accent.

It's a garden variety, pre-Bill 101 anglo accent. I struggle to get my *eu* sounds quite right—so I've been known to pronounce the city of Longueuil as "Longay"—instead of the correct *Longueueueuey*, But I read French newspapers and like most anglos I watch Canadiens hockey games on the French-language channel RDS—ever since English CBC started favoring Toronto Maple Leaf games.

Overall I think my history is typical of many, and probably most anglos. Our community has changed and adapted enormously over the past 30 years, as much as almost any in the western world. Our grandparents didn't speak French at all—they were too busy trying to survive.

But today most anglos send their kids to French immersion, or French school and many of them end up with the Québecois accent of a lumberjack and the wine sophistication of a sommelier:" *"Dad, Passe-moé le Grand Cru Château Dépanneur 2004, s'il te plaît."*

To quote a recent joke by legendary Quebec comedian Yvon Deschamps: *"On ne peut plus se moquer de nos Anglophones ... ils sont devenues bilingues .. ils nous comprennent."*

We anglos are slowly mastering many others linguistic skills too. For example we're learning to quickly decode those flashing electronic construction signs on our highways filled with large numbers of French-only words, announcing information like:

> AUTOROUTE EN CONSTRUCTION. ROUTE ALTERNATIF FACULTATIF A MONTREAL, VIA IBERVILLE par le Chemin d'Argenteuil, à la Route 66(b) et 35(a)—sujèt a des changements imprévus.

And they wonder why there's always a traffic jam on the Eastern Townships highway. It's because everyone's slowing down to read the sign—especially us anglos.

I think the roads department should at least give us some warning with a sign that says:

> "Attention! Affiche en français difficile dans 2 km. Préparez vos dictionnaires!!"

Finally there are the most challenging signs of all—Our No-Parking signs, which aren't easy to understand if you're French, let alone English. That's because they say stuff like:

> Stationnement reservé pour détenteurs du permis de residents, secteur 33, 9h à 15h et 17h à 21h—sauf les fins de semaines et jours d'écoles.

Livraison seulement—le 5 mars au 27 décembre—sauf les lun. et ven. tous les deux semaines. Rémorquage à vos frais—évidemment!

Living in Quebec is always interesting, and it's made us anglophones more interesting too. I think just like my journey from Deleppy Street to Avenue de L'Épée, we anglos have travelled a long way over the years. But it's a voyage that's just starting. The truth is that Montreal is an enigma, wrapped in a riddle, wrapped in a duffle coat. It's a mystery that's hard to fathom—and so are we anglos.

We chose to stay here when hundreds of thousands of others left. We stayed through exhausting sign law battles and two Neverendum Referendums we didn't want. We stayed because we're Québécois—and Montrealers who love our city with a passion few Canadians can outdo. We're all in favor of French signs and French service as well as French wine, French food and French kissing. That's what makes this French North America and gives our city its *je ne sais quoi*.

We've also stayed in Montreal while too many francophones have quit for the suburbs. And we may need a Bill 301 to save French in Montreal—by forbidding more francophones from moving off the island.

Like many anglos, Montreal is in my blood. It's an unpredictable, intriguing, special town—battered but beautiful, full of potholes but full of life. It's a huge laboratory where the English and French languages mix together on the street like in no other city on earth—a global experiment. It's where comedian Sugar Sammy can do a show that's half in French and half in English—and sell out to 30,000 people.

It's a city that's living proof that English and French get along very well in practice—if not in theory. With patience and time, I believe we can ultimately have a strong anglo community in a strong French Quebec; a place where the two solitudes finally become just one.

I hope our kids stay here too and master the French language well enough to achieve the impossible anglo dream—to get a job as a Quebec civil servant.

4

Snow Canada

Canadians—God's Frozen People

The British media recently declared Canada a "cool country," but they didn't realize just how accurate they were. This past winter our country has again become the wind-chill factory of the planet, the closest thing human beings have experienced to landing on Mars.

We live in a country so cold flesh freezes faster than you can get your keys out of your pocket and into the door. A place parents scream: "NO! You can't go outside and play! Get back to that TV where you belong!"

During weather like this it's only natural to become curious about our native land and ask: *Why the fuck are we Canadians here?* Let me answer your query with a brief history of Canada: Land of the Free(ze).

Question 1: Why did people first come to Canada?

They were lost. The first humans arrived here 13,000 years ago, after crossing the Bering Strait land bridge from Asia.

According to primitive ice-cave drawings, they were seeking a route to a mythical land of the gods they called "My Amee," where you could play golf and drive convertibles all year.

Unfortunately, Canadian road signs were as bad ten millennia ago as they are now, and those leading the expedition were men, who refused to ask for directions. It was only after several centuries of trudging through arctic snow that they finally admitted they had no clue where they were.

They gave up and turned back toward home. But by then, the Bering Strait was covered in water—and they were trapped on this continent, with no way back. They named their new homeland Canada: an ancient native word for "Big Mistake."

Question 2: Why did people keep coming?

In the 1500s the first French explorers crossed the Atlantic looking for Asia, but found the way blocked by rapids at Montreal. They figured China was just on the other side, which is why we still have the "Lachine Rapids."

By the time the explorers figured out where they were, winter had arrived and they were freezing their boats off. So they went charging out to hunt for furry animals to wrap themselves in. These brave hunters soon became known as *coureurs de bois*, which literally means "Running to Keep Warm."

Back in Europe, hat manufacturers somehow convinced fashionable Europeans it was cool to wear a dead beaver on your head. Thus, the Canadian fur trade was born and thrived for two centuries, selling fur to furreigners.

Over time, Canadians chased the furry rodents farther and farther inland in search of warm clothing, and accidentally explored a country. Mexico was colonized in a quest for Aztec gold; Canada in a quest to escape the cold.

Question 3: Why didn't everyone just leave?

Many French "woods-runners" did try to return home those early winters, or find a ship south to the mythical land of "Mon-ami." But winter boats were over-crowded.

Most explorers had saved up huge amounts of Fur Miles, and it was impossible to get through to a reservation agent at Canoe Canada, which was hopelessly overbooked and going bankrupt. Thus, was Canada born, a nation of trapped fur-trappers.

Gradually, those who stayed got acclimatized and became Canadian in their attitudes. Early visitors like Voltaire dismissed Canada as "a few acres of snow without a decent French restaurant for 3,000 miles." But later settlers like Champlain said: "Ah, this was just a bad winter. It will never happen again. Besides, I hear we're getting global warming in two centuries."

And so it's continued ever since, with visitors to Canada divided into two groups. One type arrives, stays a night like Voltaire and flees to someplace warmer the next day. The other type stays, grumbles all winter and then gets amnesia when summer arrives.

Complicating matters was the fact Canada used the Fahrenheit system, where water freezes at a balmy 32 degrees. This made our country sound much warmer than it was and lured many innocent immigrants, fooled by 30-degree winter temperatures as well as government of Canada photos of Banff in July.

In the 1970s, Canada finally adopted an honest advertising policy and switched over to Celsius. Suddenly, millions of Canadians were shocked to learn they had come to a country where the temperature was actually below zero most of the year.

Adding to their shock was the discovery of "wind chill" in the 1980s, which made it horribly apparent that we live on a frozen glacier blocking easy boat access between the Atlantic and Pacific oceans.

But it was too late to undo history, or move everyone to "My Amee."

Over 35 million people are now stranded on a desolate iceberg with friends, family and colleagues, living under the mass delusion that they live in a perfectly normal country. Even worse, they think they are cool. Extremely cool.

Snow Job

Winter 2008, the second snowiest in Canadian history.

Help! It's mid-winter and our city and much of our country are under siege again—by snow. Our snow banks are bigger than our buildings. Our rivers may overflow in spring, creating tidal waves, maybe even a tsno-nami.

There's no place left to put the stuff because our snow dumps are snowed in. What can we do?

Fear not—I have a plan to turn catastrophe into opportunity, if we just change our thinking. As I see it we Montrealers are now sitting on the world's largest accessible reserve of snow—another version of Calgary's oil wells. Let's stop whining about our snow and start finding ways to export our greatest natural resource. Let's sell our snow to the world!

Why not? Newfoundland craftily tows away its dirty old icebergs, then sells them worldwide for a fortune to nations eager to make "10,000-year-old iceberg martinis." In Europe, every third-rate brook-side village bottles its scuzzy town water as "pristine Alpine mountain spring nectar drawn from the mystic evergreen glades."

It's time Quebecers and other snowed-in Canadians showed the same marketing skills to get our white stuff off our streets—tand balconies—and into someone else's hands. Just look at our potential customers! Let's start by exporting to the obvious buyers—those oil-rich Middle East emirates that are desperate for the stuff.

Dubai and Bahrain have spent a fortune building giant indoor ski hills, but they're using second-rate artificial snow, when we have mountains of the real stuff to offer—without even denting our reserves. We could ship it by the tanker, in ready-made ski hills, or sell it by the barrel—or even by the individual snowflake. Whatever the packaging, we'd send them a ship full of snow and they'd send one back filled with oil.

Many other countries are crying for our white stuff, too—tropical islands where snow-starved children dream of a white Christmas they've only seen on TV. All we have to do is load up a fleet of Hercules military cargo planes with refrigerated fresh powder, then swoop over the villages and bomb them with a blizzard of snow.

I can imagine the kids rushing from their homes in bare feet to greet their first snowstorm, excitedly pointing at the sky and shouting: "Look! White magic—from Canada!" Christmas orders would be huge everywhere from Jamaica and the Sahara to rainy Holland—but we could handle the demand easily. Our current snow reserve fields are at record levels—and our product is so renewable not even global warming can stop it.

As demand for our product rises, so will our price, creating a new snow economy. We can build giant snow pipelines to transport our crude stuff directly from our snowfields to water-parched countries where they'll filter, refine and drink it. We can become "white desert sheiks." We'd have skilled winter workers from all over Canada lined up looking for a high-paying snow job.

Eventually with the rising price of snowflakes Montreal streets won't have a drop of precious snow left on them. Not to mention all the spin-off business. Many countries don't have the clothing or equipment to enjoy snow properly, so we could provide them with the whole winter package—from snow shovels and snow tires to parkas, mitts and long underwear.

I can hear the head of Montreal's Snow Exporting Department reporting, as business pours in. "We're snowed under with orders, boss. We just got a request for 50,000 barrels of pure powder snow from Saudi Arabia and another 30,000 of crude balcony and school-roof snow from Tahiti.

"Dubai wants a 2.7 billion-flake blizzard by Friday for their royal birthday party—and they'll take 200,000 mittens, tuques and neck-warmers, too. Things are crazy here, snow joke."

With every delivery, we'd send in large teams of expert snow consultants to instruct new customers on how to use our product properly. Which experts? Any average Canadian will do. We'll teach our foreign customers how to ski in snow, walk in snow, drive in it, shovel it, leap over it and complain about it. Then when they've finally had enough of it— like us—we can rent them our snowplows, snowblowers and snow teams to get rid of it.

They can even celebrate winter's end with a new world-famous drink we'll invent to compete with Newfoundland's iceberg martinis. Anyone for a Montreal "scotch and snowda?"

Canadian Climate Clash

It's taking forever to write this because I keep gazing out the window at another gorgeous August day and wondering if I should stop working. Maybe I'm missing the Last Nice Day of Summer? Maybe I should go out and take a bike ride, or just a siesta in the park? Then again, maybe I should just stare out the window and think about it some more.

I'm one of 37 million Canadians suffering from Summer Sun Syndrome, caused by several hot months that slow my brain to the speed of a sparrow's. It turns me into a totally different person than I am the rest of the year.

Here in Canada we live in one of the world's most extreme climates, with blistering tropical summers and frigid arctic winters that give many of us a seasonal Jekyll and Hyde split personality. Part of us is Summer Canadian, the other part Winter Canadian—and they couldn't be more different, because while they share the same body, they live in utterly opposite climates.

Winter Canadian is a pale, stressed-out creature bundled in five layers of clothing who lives in the High Arctic. This creature is always in a rush, hurrying from one warm place to the next, its mind whirling with things to do: leap over a snow bank, unfreeze the car lock, smash the ice off the windshield then drive the kids to a hockey practice two hours away in a blinding snowstorm.

In contrast, *Summer Canadian* is a tanned, blissed-out personality who ambles the streets lazily, its mind a blank. This creature lives in a steamy tropical climate, like last week's heat wave, when it was so humid pigeons were falling from the sky with heat stroke and squirrels were spontaneously combusting and bursting into flame.

Summer Canadian talks slowly, walks slower and even drives slower than Winter Canadian because—hey, what's the hurry? This personality stops to admire pretty cloud formations, or a lovely sliver of moon that Winter Canadians never notice, because they're too busy looking down so they won't slip on the ice.

Winter Canadian is also a conscientious global citizen who devours TV news and newspapers to keep its mind off its own difficult existence. The typical Winter Canadian knows the weekly casualty count in Syria, the latest power struggles in Washington and France and all the nightly hockey scores.

Summer Canadian couldn't care less. It's a vacuous creature with little interest in anything but barbecuing, salad recipes and finding a good rosé. It's an intellectual midget who barely watches the news—he knows there's none anyway, because the politicians are all on vacation—and he wishes they'd stay there.

Summer Canadian is an exercise fanatic who walks, bikes, swims, plays tennis and sits on outdoor *terrasses* doing beer-mug lifts. But Winter Canadian is a lazy creature whose only exercise is dressing for thirty minutes to go outside.

As a result Winter Canada weighs 35 million pounds more than Summer Canada. Make that 37 million if you include winter clothes. That's because Winter Canadian dresses in seven layers of clothing and doesn't see himself naked for six months a year. Meanwhile, Summer Canadian just has a pair of shorts, or a short skirt—and sandals—and figures no one cares. If summer lasted long enough, we'd all become nudists.

At heart, Winter Canadian is a feverish 24/7 workaholic because there's nothing to do in winter, except work, ski or rush out to move the car when the snow clearing sirens wail. In contrast, Summer Canadian goes to work as late as possible, has a long outdoor *terrasse* lunch and returns to the office utterly drained from the heat, to spend the rest of the day gazing out the window, wondering if it's time to start working. If it weren't for Winter Canadian, our province's economy would be worse than Greece's.

Above all, Summer Canadian is a friendly type who loves to yak on the street with neighbors, friends, passersby and winos. He'll spend hours on a street corner talking to someone he hasn't seen for ages, until he suddenly realizes he doesn't actually know them. Yet he keeps on talking anyway, because by then he does know them.

Winter Canadian is an introverted creature who can go all winter without talking to their next door neighbors. That's because they don't recognize them under their parkas and hoods. If Winter Canadian ever met Summer Canadian, conversation would be awkward.

SUMMER CANADIAN: Hey—how're ya doing! You new on this block?

WINTER CANADIAN: Actually, I've lived here thirty years. It's nice to meet you—but I'm a little busy now, so maybe we could chat tonight after work, once I get out of my health club at 7:30, then spend twenty minutes dressing and thirty minutes stressing in traffic. Now excuse me while I go dig out my car.

SUMMER CANADIAN: Hey man, what's the rush? Life is short and beautiful ... let's go find a *terrasse* and chill out.

WINTER CANADIAN: I am chilled man—it's minus 22.

So there they are, Dr. Goof-off of Canadian summer and Mr. Hide from Canadian winter. They are both us—and me. And now, since it's summer, it's time to goof off.

The Olympic Games People Play

[Summer, 2008]

It's Olympics time again, when we gather on our couches to watch the world's best athletes run like the wind, swim like fish, leap like gazelles and give urine samples like gang members caught in a drug bust.

There are gymnasts defying gravity on the high bars, the rings and the kinky pommel horse. There are infinite numbers of swimming races from the 200 meter to the 250 meter to the 251 meter and 251.5687 meter. But how does any of this relate to our daily lives? Most of us can't do one chin-up, let alone a quadruple midair somersault followed by a double-Stutz, triple- Tkatchev, reverse-Timonchenk-Yurchenko vault.

Many sports like javelin-throwing and archery are antiquated relics of our hunting days, while swimming and running are leftover skills from fleeing from our predators. The only place we ever run today is on a treadmill—or maybe to catch a bus.

Yet 21st century life *is* filled with thrilling modern skills we excel at, using remarkable new talents we've developed to confront today's challenges. It's time these skills were reflected in a new global competition—The Real Summer Olympics—where humanity would compete in contests that measure our true modern worth. For instance:

The 3,000-Metre Supermarket Sprint: In this event, athletes would race through a giant supermarket, shopping for a family of five. Important skills tested would include quickly comparing 55 brands of cereal ingredients to see which is healthy, edible and affordable. Also, trying to choose orange juice among endless rows of the stuff offered with pulp, without pulp, with partial pulp or with organic, pulp-enhanced supplement fortified with Vitamin D and fish oil.

Judges would award points for economy shopping as well as doing your own swiping and bagging, while penalties would be assessed for missing a supermarket flyer special, or trying to sneak into the five-items-or-less line. Imagine the thrilling play-by-play commentary:

> ANNOUNCER 1: "Hello sports fans. If you're just joining us, Carla Hodgson of Red Deer, Alberta is just reaching the cereal section in the supermarket sprint—and she quickly goes for the corn flakes marked down by 30 per cent, when you buy two boxes. But now her youngest daughter is complaining—she wants the Rice Krispies instead—at full price!
> ANNOUNCER 2: Ohmigod Brian!— now her other daughter has started to cry. Carla looks agitated ... she's turning back for the Rice Krispies and—ohhh!—she drops the corn flakes! That will cost her a second of time—and the judges may deduct style points too.
> ANNOUNCER 1: You're right, Pam—the only way Carla can make up her lost time now is by guessing the fastest check-out line. Wow, this is a nail-biter!"

Calculate the Real-air-Fare Race: Competitors must estimate the real cost of a $159 airline "seat sale" to Hong Kong, "not including taxes and other fees." They must calculate the seat selection fee, luggage fee, meal surcharge, fuel charge, long distance special fuel surcharge, audio headphone purchase price, seat reclining fee, eating utensil surcharge, oxygen mask access fee, airport departure tax, arrival tax and special landing fee if you plan to stay more than 20 minutes.

Also GST, QST, VAT, MSG and "I'd rather take the TGV."

Multi-tasking Decathlon: Competitors must drive downtown in rush hour traffic while simultaneously talking on the cellphone, changing radio stations, adjusting the air-conditioner, programming the GPS, eating a large unsliced pizza, drinking a grande frappuccino, sending emails and flossing their teeth.

Points are deducted for traffic tickets, accidents and food stains.

Ultimately the Real Summer Olympics would be more entertaining and relevant than our current games and serve a larger global purpose. Instead of encouraging youngsters to sacrifice 15 long years learning how to throw a javelin, or play volleyball in a bikini, these games would inspire kids to develop useful, real-life skills that would last forever. In fact we could do the same for the Real Winter Games too with events like:

The Competitive Car Dig-Out: In this grueling sport, competitors confront cars that have been buried in snow and ice by passing snow trucks. At the gun, athletes must shovel the wheels out of frozen snow banks, pound their way through an inch of windshield ice, then instantly decide whether to use salt, sand, a claw or cat litter for traction.

Finally, athletes must rock the car from behind while barking commands to a driver, like: "Forward, forward! STOP! Straighten your wheels. Easy on the gas. NO! Don't spin your tires!! God! Someone call CAA!"

Olympic Ball Hockey: Forget indoor hockey on perfectly groomed ice. How about a challenging game of ball hockey, on a busy car-filled street like Park Ave. where players have to keep one eye on the ball and the other out for speeding cabs, trucks and bike couriers? The play-by-play commentary would be thrilling:

"Rabuski has the ball. He dekes between two parked cars. He leaps a snow bank! He's in on net! And *ohhhhh*—he's mowed down by the 80 bus!"

Storm Morning Mom Marathon: Teams of mothers would compete to dress ten kids in five layers of clothing that keep them warm, but not so warm they'll sweat on the metro, then freeze when they step outside. Contestants would be scored on skill but also on style, like figure-skaters. Do the kids look warm and cool at the same time?

Everyday Triathlon: Three strenuous back-to-back events. First, the 60-step icy spiral staircase downhill run, then the carry-seven-packages out of the car with both hands full across sheer ice, followed by snowbank hurdling. Finally, the post-dinner-and-drinks 500-yard sprint to move the car after you suddenly hear the snow sirens. Medals are awarded to the three first competitors to find a new parking spot. Losers must circle the block for hours.

Like the Summer Games, every small country would have a chance to win all these events because there'd be no money or equipment needed—just the true Olympic winter spirit, expressed by the motto: The Winter Games: Colder, Wetter, Sicker.

Err Canada

I recently joined a special airline club. It's not the usual Super Elite Pomp and Prestige Aeroplan Privileged High-Flyer Program. No, I belong to the 4-Star Sucker's Frequent-Flyer-Without-Luggage Plan.

And I earned my stars the hard way.

I got my first star seven weeks ago when I took a KLM flight abroad for work and my bags didn't show up for 24 hours. I earned my second star when I flew back home and my bags arrived four days later.

So you can imagine how I felt when I flew to Italy on holiday two weeks ago and landed in Rome—without my luggage again. That's three trips out of four without my suitcase—why do I bother packing it?

I prowled around the Rome airport for two hours in disbelief, then lined up at the lost luggage counter to collect my third star. The Air Canada agents gave me a reference code and a local phone number to call and promised they'd contact me quickly with news. But that's the last I heard of them.

I spent the next few days frenetically phoning their Rome office, trying to reach a human. All I got was an automated phone machine that asked me to punch in my reference code, then put me on hold for 10 minutes before emitting the same terse electronic message, in Italian and English.

"*Beep.* File FCO AC11208. Bag still untraced. Goodbye. Arrividerci." Then it hung up.

After three days of this treatment, I became convinced that there was no Air Canada Rome office, just a machine sitting in a field near the Coliseum, repeating the same recording. I spent those days without any clothing, increasingly angry at my national airline.

In recent years, like many carriers, they have whittled away much of their staff and outsourced their jobs to us passengers. We now make our own reservations on the Internet, then print our own boarding passes at the airport. We undress ourselves at the security gate and in recent months we're being taught how to tag our own baggage.

For all I know, that's why my bag was missing in Rome—as a novice tagger I'd mistakenly sent it to India instead of Italy.

I'm a great fan of Air Canada's hard-working, highly professional staff, but there are fewer and fewer of them around to serve us. What next? Will they teach us to cook our own in-flight chicken—or to de-ice the planes? And why stop there?

"Attention passengers! Welcome aboard Air Canada flight 374 with Superplus Automated No-Pilot service to Calgary. Please consult your electronic console to chart your personalized flight course home."

Meanwhile, back in Rome, it was Day 4 and Air Canada was still training me to trace my own luggage—which didn't leave much time for holidays. Over several days I had called their Rome "office" 40 times, pressed 1,500 phone keys and spent several hours on hold. I was financing this luggage search, too.

I was living in a small Italian village with no available telephone, so all my calls to Rome were made long distance on my own cellphone, going Italy-Canada-Italy at God knows what price. And I had other bills too.

On the fifth day, my luggage finally showed up, but by then I'd bought a whole new wardrobe of skin-tight Italian T-shirts and skimpy underwear that cost 30 euros a pair. Like most travellers, I'd carefully packed my holiday luggage to cope with the unpredictable winter weather of Italy.

Who knew I'd be wearing one Polo shirt all week?

For the record, more headaches awaited on my flight home. My luggage didn't show up in Toronto for an hour after the other bags, so I had to run an Olympic dash to catch my Montreal connection— where my Rome duty-free liquor was seized by security staff. But I won't bore you with such routine details of flying today.

Let's just say that by the time I'd stepped into Montreal airport, 45 minutes ahead of my luggage, I'd come to a conclusion. Next time I fly somewhere, even if it's for a year, I'll pack everything I want in my carry-on bag and leave my suitcase at home.

Airlines don't really do baggage anymore—or much else. Self-service is the future of flying and I'm better off doing the luggage-handling myself.

Meanwhile, I'm still waiting for that Rome phone bill to arrive—which will probably cost more than my airline ticket. In fact, several days after I received my bag, I made one more long-distance call to Air Canada's Rome "office," just out of curiosity.

According to the machine, my luggage was still missing.

The Great Canadian UpNorth

School's out, July's here and it's time for that age-old summer ritual—going to "the country."

To newcomers and tourists "the country" conjures up the rugged Canadian wilderness, where hardy Canucks portage canoes, sleep in lean-tos and leg-wrestle grizzly bears. But to veterans, "the country" just means going to the cottage for the weekend, to stew in traffic, get bitten by insects and leap into water cold enough to freeze fish.

For you beginners, here is a Rough Guide to "The Country":

How do I find the country?

Take the nearest highway from your city and drive 93 kilometres in any direction—then get off at the second exit after the Tim Horton's, or the *La Belle Province* hot dog sign. Stay on the small winding road for nine kilometers until it turns to dirt and there are no signs—but don't worry. Just keep on driving till you pass the old barn that's not there anymore because it burned down.

Watch carefully for the first right after the second gravel road after the third cottage, where you'll see a small invisible driveway—then pull in at the small log cabin. That's the garage and your host will come down to greet you in his four-wheeler.

How long does the trip take?

Your hosts will say "it takes exactly 63 minutes," but like physicists they mean theoretically, in a vacuum—in perfect weather, with no accidents, or construction, or wind, or other cars on the road.

These conditions never happen, so it will take you three hours in bumper-to-bumper construction traffic, with 500,000 other city people all trying to get there in 63 minutes—and ready to kill to arrive five car lengths before you.

If traffic is really bad, most men take a detour on a meandering 50-kilometre dirt road that goes the wrong way and is crowded with other male drivers desperately looking for a detour. Guys are happy as long as they're moving, but women prefer to stay on the highway and wait the traffic out.

They are obviously insane. When women drive you get to the country in 1.4 hours, but it feels like forever. When guys drive, it feels like thirty minutes, though it's taken three hours.

What is the "cottage"?

Traditionally the cottage was a wood shack with cold water, no phone and two cots that sagged—but now that would be shut down by health inspectors. Today's cottage has a dishwasher, microwave, satellite TV, Internet, Jenn-Air, Aga stove and a pool beside the lake.

Studies show 47 per cent of Canadians do enter the lake as far as their toes. Another 35 per cent wade to their knees, while 18 per cent submerge their bodies. Children are harder to get in, because they say things like: "Oh, it's muddy! I-iccckkk! I want blue water like the pool!"

But eventually, they always go in and refuse to come out until they turn blue.

Is there any wildlife?

The city may be empty of wildlife, but in the country you still see many fierce creatures—such as the deer(fly), the horse(fly) and even the dragon(fly).

Throw in the blackfly, the house fly, mosquitoes, wasps, hornets and West Nile no-see-ums—and there's way more wildlife than you want. Savvy country veterans cover their bodies in D.E.E.T and wear strips of fabric softener hanging from their hats, belts and socks. The bugs don't bite as much because they're too busy laughing.

(For more details see "Battle of the Bug" below)

So what exactly do you do in the country?

On Saturday, you talk about the weather—how wet, or damp, or humid it is. That night, you stand on the deck and say stuff like: "Red sky at night, sailors' delight"—just before you run in because it's raining.

Sunday morning you compare bites: "Ohmigod look at me!—I'm disfigured! HAS ANYONE GOT SOME BOTOX?!" By noon, you start anxiously debating whether you should leave early and beat all the traffic going in that evening. The next four hours are spent in the car, complaining about the traffic, because everyone else decided to leave early and beat the traffic, too.

Battle of the Bug

Here in the city there is skirmishing, but *UpNorth* in the country there is all-out bloodshed. It is bug season, pitting mankind against mosquito—and country patios run red with the blood of the Canadian cottager.

Global warming might be bad for people and polar bears but it's great for our bugs, which thrive on our recent wet springs and hot summers—ideal mating conditions over at Club Med For Mosquitoes. "Did'ja hear, Bugsy? Canada's got fabulous weather this year. Everyone's heading North for the summer—that's the buzz."

Canadian entomologists say we have three times as many biting bugs in recent years. Last month the mosquitoes on my balcony got so vicious they actually scared off the pigeons. But no place has been as savagely hit as "the country," which has turned into a killing field—from "UpNorth" to "WayupNorth." On almost every front, the enemy includes the same list of combatants.

THE MOSQUITO: This is the shark of the air, a bloodthirsty carnivore that loves a hearty barbecue—and you are the menu. Mosquitoes have been feasting on people for millennia, though we know more about them now than we did when they devastated the ancient Romans. Scientists have discovered these bugs prefer pale-skinned people with fair hair and dark clothing—and they're especially drawn to the smell of old cheese and smelly toes. So their favorite meal is a blonde with dirty feet eating a cheeseburger.

THE DEERFLY: This large fly-like creature has the IQ of an axe handle, and drones about your head like a B-52. Yet its buzz is not as bad as its bite.

While a mosquito treats you like a milkshake, deerflies see you as a Big Mac—and when they bite you, it feels like they've just swallowed a Quarter Pounder. This bug is too stupid to flee, even after you howl with pain and swat at it —so you can kill it easily—but reinforcements will arrive minutes later and demand another quarter-pound of flesh.

THE BLACKFLY: This is the pit bull of the insect world, a tiny creature that sucks big time and leaves a bite the size of a watermelon. Like motorcycle gangs, they travel in swarms and love gratuitous bloodshed. They are often accompanied by microscopic bugs called "no-see-ums"—though unfortunately they see you, and you feel 'em.

THE REST OF THE PESTS: To add to the action there are humongous horseflies that tear the flesh off your body, sadistic wasps that sting just for kicks and suicidal bees that will sacrifice their lives for a sting operation. There are also creepy-looking things like dragonflies that don't even have to bite. They scare you to death by appearance alone. The least violent of the bunch is our early childhood terror, the bumblebee, which turns out to be a gentle Disney-like creature—the Bambi of the bug world—that never stings unless attacked. Like most of our bugs she's an annoying but ultimately civilized Canadian that wounds but never kills.

In response we humans fight back with an arsenal of sprays like 6-12 and Off—which most bugs consider an hors d'oeuvre before the main course. We also use heavy artillery, from D.E.E.T. to toxic coils to electric swatters and zappers that fry bugs alive—entomology's answer to the electric chair.

But it's all futile. Our bugs are as resilient a piece of Canadian life as our snow and slush—and they don't get their due in Canadian mythology. Look at the coins in your pocket and you'll see the caribou, the loon and the beaver—but honestly, when was the last time you saw one of these creatures in real life?

It's time our national symbols reflected our daily lives and the challenges we face trying to enjoy a simple summer weekend. Let's put a deer fly on the quarter, a blackfly on the nickel and a no-see-um on the dime. Let's replace the Maple Leaf with a symbol that actually means something to us: a huge red mosquito, swollen with the blood of all Canadians. At last, we'd have a national symbol with bite.

No Labor Day

Happy Labor Day weekend, everyone! I'm sure you're celebrating by roasting a Labor Day turkey, or painting some Labor Day eggs—or putting your family's gifts under the Labor Day tree.

Sorry to belabor your day, but how exactly are we supposed to celebrate this holiday, apart from sitting on our balcony and drinking beer? We all know why we mark Thanksgiving, Christmas, Canada Day and St. Jean—but few of us know why we do not labor on Labor Day.

The yearly event is the Pluto of statutory holidays, a mysterious long weekend that would probably lose its holiday status if we ever studied it too carefully.

To start with, most of us assume that Labor Day marks the end of summer holidays—the signal to go back to work, back to school and back to too-much-traffic and not-enough-parking spaces. But that's not true anymore. In our new work-obsessed world, most kids have been back slaving at school ever since late August—they are the new working "class." In fact Labor Day has now become a strangely out-of-synch school holiday that interrupts the first week of classes and teachers' efforts to learn their students' names.

Back to work? Sorry—over 40 per cent of Americans took no summer holiday at all last year, while a quarter of Canadians took very little or none. In Europe, people still take four to six weeks of summer holidays but here the meager traditional two-week holiday is now shrinking fast. Even when we do take holidays, we are umbilically tied to our workplace by email and voice mail. How can you go back to work when you never leave it?

Even those North Americans who did manage to take a summer holiday mostly followed their kids back to work last week. In the Workaholic World, August has become the new September, and at the rate we're working it will soon become July. Maybe we should just move Labor Day back a week or two to mid-August, where it belongs. Or maybe we could postpone it to February when we really need a break. Why do we have to celebrate Labor Day in September, anyway?

The truth is that Labor Day has been held then ever since the late 1800s, when workers in Canada and the United States marched in the streets demanding shorter work hours. Officially, Labor Day honors laborers, although this too seems increasingly outdated. Most of the world now celebrates workers on May 1st—known as May Day—when worldwide protests take place. A September Labor Day holiday takes place only in Canada and the U.S., where the name is a mystery to most.

I suppose it's better than celebrating International Bosses' Day. But the reality is not that many Canadians actually labor for a living anymore in today's information age. Fewer and fewer of us swing a pickaxe, or push a plough. Instead, we toil at typing. We send emails. We yack on the phone. And most of us continue to do exactly the same things on Labor Day when we are off the job, but voluntarily sitting at our computers, blurring the line between work and leisure.

Meanwhile, many remaining laborers who really need a Labor Day break don't get one. Civil servants and union workers get the day off but McDonald's staff will be working Monday, along with gas jockeys, cabbies and many other laborers who don't get paid to celebrate Labor Day. Not to mention any mothers who go into labor on Labor Day.

Maybe it's time to reinvent this holiday to suit the digital age, instead of the industrial age. We used to dream of becoming a leisure society with endless free time, but instead work has become our modern religion, while taking a long vacation is often seen as heresy, or slacking off.

If anything we need a new holiday called "No Labor day," or "Leisure Day," when no one is allowed to work, or type, or telephone or study—and when stores, supermarkets and even the Holy Internet are all officially "Closed For the Day." It would be an annual day of rest from all labor, much like Sunday used to be, before we made it our biggest shopping day and another chance to catch up on work.

In fact, why don't we call the new annual holiday "Sunday"? Then we could rename Sunday something more modern and appropriate—like Labor Day.

Rebranding Global Warming

You should be very worried about our wonderful warm weather—especially if you read last week's cover story in *Time* magazine. It's a scary Special Report On Global Warming, with the headline "BE WORRIED. BE VERY WORRIED."

So why aren't we? Here in Montreal we've had the warmest, freakiest fall in memory, after an unusually perfect summer, after a bizarrely warm winter, and the warmer it gets, the happier we are. Yes, I know the polar caps are melting and tiny islands are sinking, while Florida may end up under water. But I can't help but like the heat, whatever's causing it.

Worse, I'm typical of many Canadians. Despite massive media coverage of global warming most of us aren't reacting with real alarm. We drive SUVs, we air-condition until we freeze in summer, then heat till we sweat in winter. Why aren't we more frightened of global warming? Could it be the term itself just doesn't sound scary?

The fact is "warming" isn't really a negative word. A cold front sounds scary, but a warm one doesn't. The Cold War was a frightening thought, while a Warm War isn't. An Ice Age sounds bad, while a Heat Age sounds like a beach holiday. Everyone likes warm people, warm lunches, hot dogs and hot dates. No one likes cold people, cold showers or catching a cold.

Sadly, marketing matters even when it comes to disasters. The Black Plague still resonates, partly because it was well-named (and partly because it decimated Europe). Mad Cow disease is also an excellent scary name that helped get Canadian cows banned from the States, far better than just calling it Bovine Spongiform Encephalopathy.

Even avian flu is scary, because it sounds like it's swooping down on you. As a kid the Asian Flu terrified me because it sounded alien—but as the world becomes smaller, it doesn't. It just sounds like an industrious flu that works long hours at a call center. Maybe it's time to rebrand global warming with a more terrifying name, one that creates fear in the pit of our stomachs, like the sound of a dentist's drill.

The U.S. is good at making real menaces sound even more menacing—just look at the War on Crime, the War on Drugs and the War on Terror. We need an American-style rebranding campaign for global warming, too. Here are some suggestions:

1) Even the simplest spelling change could turn global warming into something creepier—like global harming. Or global warring. It worked for Nuclear War, which terrified us for 50 years.

2) Diseases are also frightening these days as we worry about bird flu, swine flu and a return of the great 1918 killer flu pandemic. What if we made the planet's problems sound more like a sickness, with actual germs that people could get paranoid about? For instance, we could invent a scary new disease like "global killer climate flu," or "global planetary plague." We could also try global cancer—there's a word that always scares people, transforming chronic drinkers and smokers into tea-totalers.

A name with a creepy acronym would also be good, like Defective International Epidemic Syndrome (DIES). Or Sick Universe Virus (SUV).

3) The word "terror" instantly creates fear about anything connected to it, from terror alerts and terrorist cells to biological terrorists and computer terrorists. Calling the problem "global climate terror" would definitely get everyone's attention, even Stephen Harper might sign the Kyoto Accord overnight.

4) The word "global" isn't really that scary, either. Perhaps it would be better if we found a more creepy-sounding term, like "alien climate flu,." Or "evil planet virus." Or "Satanic planet syndrome." If we put them all together we'd really have something to worry about. I can already see the cover of Time warning us about "Satanic Alien Evil Planetary Terror Mad Plague Climate Syndrome."

Now I'm getting worried.

Canada Day Hooray!

[July 1, 2010]

According to a poll last week, the whole world wants to abandon their countries and move to ours, which would give us a population of four billion—and the rest of Earth three billion. Over half the people in the world's top 24 economies want to immigrate here, while China and India would practically empty out, ending the Chinese over-population crisis and creating a Canadian one.

But why shouldn't they want to come to Canada? Most of these nations have never actually lived through a Canadian winter—and their doctors, lawyers, professors, rocket scientists and movie stars don't know they'd have to become cabbies when they got here. They don't know Stephen Harper is going to spend $10 billion on jails—and then create criminals to fill them.

So I understand their desire to be Canadian. Whenever I travel Canada always looks great from far—and that's how most of the world always sees us. But as well, Canada's reputation is on a real roll.

Just a few years ago, our loonie had sunk so low there was talk of renaming it the "puny", but now it's flying so high it may someday become the real dollar of North America. Our banks are the envy of every country since the 2008 recession, in fact they are now the biggest banks in the world—because most of the other big banks are gone.

Our Canadian passport has become the most prized document on earth for crossing any border—recommended by every Russian arms dealer and nine out of ten terrorists. Even our oldest, coldest curse is lifting—our weather—as global warming gradually opens up Canada's Northwest Passage. This could eventually create a new Arctic Riviera, with Canada's answer to France's famed coastal city, *Nice*—only ours would be pronounced Nice.

When I was a kid, we were repeatedly told "the 20th century belongs to Canada," a famous line by Wilfrid Laurier. Instead, we suffered through decades of constitutional trauma and neverendum referendum nausea as the century passed us by. In the '90s, we lived through the "brain drain" and watched our sports teams, like the Expos and the Nordiques flee to the U.S. There were rumors Team Canada might defect to Miami. There was even a brief clamor to merge our dollar and our country with the United States.

But in recent years everything has turned around. Today Canada looks so good, even the United States has elected a Canadian-style leader—"No-drama" Obama, who fought to bring in a pale version of our Medicare system. Sure we face challenges. Our high-flying dollar is killing Hollywood North, as American film crews go home and Canadian movies start shooting in Los Angeles, to take advantage of the low U.S. dollar.

But eventually we should be able to finance our own Canadian film blockbusters—all documentaries—like *The Codfather, and Gone with the WindChill, a*nd the Canadian version of *The Ten Commandments*—renamed "*The Ten Suggestions.*"

According to that poll of nations last week, foreigners told pollsters they see Canada as a very friendly, polite and somewhat dull country — but not a sexy one. And that's why they want to come here. The truth is most of the world would love to be as polite, boring and safe as us.

So I say, dare to dream, Canadians. *Dare* to be dull. Don't go wild—go mild! It's time for a new Canadian-style planet with think tanks instead of real tanks, where we don't reach for our holsters, we reach for our pollsters. A world where there are no more warring nations, only boring nations—like us.

So have a happy and boring Canada Day everyone!

5

Like So Yesterday

Quest for Fire-Starter

In summer, like most men I get a deep primordial urge to char meat black over an open flame.

Many women like their barbecues too, but they see them as just another kitchen appliance, like the food processor or the electric cake-mixer. But guys have a special love affair with their barbecues, including many who don't know how to make Kraft Dinner.

Why do men embrace this clunky, old-fashioned machine? Partly it's because we love fiddling with the coals, the wood chips—or the propane valve. We love the grease, the grit, the char, the smoke, the sizzle and especially the flame, which occasionally bursts into the air and makes cooking seem almost dangerous.

It is our quest for fire-starter.

As well, the barbecue is the only remaining gadget that isn't run by computer chips—you actually light the coals yourself, or push the gas starter button and *whoosh* ... FIRE! Usually the button doesn't work so you have to light the flame with an actual match—something guys don't get to handle much anymore, now that cigarettes are becoming history.

I've always thought the barbecue was secretly invented by women to trick stove-challenged men into cooking. If they came up with a gadget to wash the dishes over an open fire, men would enjoy dishwashing so much they'd name beer brands after detergents—like "Suds." In fact, if they invented a way to vacuum the halls with a flame-thrower, men would take over the housework completely.

There just aren't many places left anymore where we can exercise our Inner Guy by fussing with machinery, since most modern gadgets are too complicated to mess with. When I was growing up every guy was a Mr. Fix-it, even if he didn't know anything—because most gadgets didn't work unless you fiddled with them.

In our house, the black-and-white TV always had a flickering picture—and my dad's job was to move the "rabbit ears" around, or adjust the "vertical hold" knob until the picture straightened out. Real men didn't even touch the knobs; they just pounded on top of the TV—which usually worked.

It made you feel way more useful than today, when you lie in a La-Z-Boy clicking the remote to adjust the already perfect color balance. The inside of my flat-screen plasma TV might as well be a nuclear reactor it's so unfathomable—if there even is anything inside that thin-as-a-credit-card screen.

A car is another thing that no longer allows much fiddling. In my twenties I took an auto mechanics course and learned the names of all the parts I couldn't fix. "Yup—looks like the starter solenoid shorting out the bell-housing sump-pump widget-wonker and the gasket seal camshaft nimrod torque ring."

But now the car's getting so computerized you'll soon need a degree in electronics to change the windshield fluid. You can't even fix something minor like the carburetor anymore—you have to go to the garage where they'll just replace the entire fuel-injection system because the mechanic doesn't know how to fix it either.

About the only chance you get to fiddle with anything is when you phone the cable company or the phone company which don't actually come to your house to fix anything. They just tell *you* how to fix it.

"Okay, sir. If you could just check the connection between the small black wire and the small red one."

"Uh … but the black cable leads out my apartment window onto the seventh floor ledge."

"Perfect, sir, that's where it should be. Now just climb out on the ledge, then reach up near the roof for a red wire with two metal leads. But don't touch the power line!"

The latest vanishing skill is finding your way around, as GPS navigation systems tell you exactly how to get somewhere without knowing where you are. Map-reading will soon be as quaint as writing with a quill, and, eventually, you won't even understand when someone says: "Go to the second intersection and take the third left."

Instead you'll wonder: "What's a *left*?"

Of course, we do have some modern skills our ancestors didn't. We can punch phone buttons and order take-out. We use iPhones and send emails—and some people can even assemble IKEA shelving. And of course, we all pump our own gas—at today's prices, even the Queen probably pumps gas.

Meanwhile, we men cling to the barbecue, the last place a guy can feel genuinely useful by turning a few dials and banging the grill cover shut. But I don't know how long that will last. Already I hear guys whining that they'd like an electronic BBQ timer that dings like a microwave when the food is ready, so you don't have to stay out on the balcony in the cold.

Soon they'll invent a remote-control barbecue so you can adjust the heat from the living room while watching the football game, and monitoring the flame on part of your TV screen. Eventually the BBQ Safety Police will decide that live flame is dangerous and "Grills Kill"—and they'll make us convert to an electronic flame that does virtual barbecuing.

When barbecues vanish, men will retreat to the last place they still feel manly—doing the dishes on their flame-throwing dishwasher.

We've All Been Framed!

I went to a concert recently where half the crowd wasn't watching the band—they were watching their cellphones, while they took pictures of the band. It was typical of our photographic new world where we view life through the viewfinder.

There was a time not so long ago when we took most of our photos at family gatherings or birthdays—and people even dressed up for the occasion. But in recent years we shoot ourselves doing pretty much anything—so we can email the shots to our friends, under subject headings like: "Photo of Josh buying milk. Photo of Josh parking car. Photo of Josh taking photos."

Life is one big photo op, from your first ultrasound womb-cam shots to the funeral-cam that broadcasts your death "live" on the Web. Every school play and concert is now captured on 300 cameras, by parents who don't really pay any attention to the show until they're watching it later at home. At the Louvre, few people study the Mona Lisa anymore—they just shoot her to watch later in pale video, instead of rich oil colors.

Billions of photos are now snapped on cellphones every year—so many that photographs should really be renamed "phone-ographs." Everyone is armed and ready to record every last frame of life. If you slip on a banana peel, don't count on anyone helping you up—they'll be too busy shooting you for *The World's Funniest Falling on A Banana Peel* show.

No matter what the disaster someone with a video camera is around, filming the victims instead of helping them. If you're about to crash your plane, or car it's wise to look your best at the last second, because someone will be there to film you, then send the video off to www.carcrash.com, where it will be the last shots you are remembered by—possibly seen by millions of people.

So remember to smile.

We used to worry that Big Brother was watching us with an all-seeing eye, but it turns out we are all Big Brother, watching each other. Get too drunk at a party and pictures of it will be on the Web before you even get home. We are a nation of paparazzi—happily destroying our own privacy.

Who'd have imagined it? When I grew up the camera was still a magic box whose often over-exposed pictures seemed so precious we even kept the blurry ones. They captured unexpected real moments where your hair was over your eyes, or your mouth hung open because you'd smiled a second before the camera went off—and you didn't find out until you got the roll back from the "developer."

But digital cameras have changed that by allowing us to delete-and-reshoot the same picture endless times until we get the perfect pose, perfect smile and perfect light. Any photo with a goofy smile, or your mouth open can be erased instantly—then replaced with another "great photo" of you with a fabulous smile that's so perfect it's not much fun to look at.

Why even bother to say "cheese"? You can make yourself smile later with Photoshop's "Say Cheese" software program. You can erase all wrinkles, crinkles, creases and smirks, or eliminate unwanted spouses, parents, guests and kids from the shot—using the Stalin Airbrush Effect. You can nostalgize over your 25th anniversary photos without being reminded of your husband, because you "photo-chopped" the S.O.B. out of the event when you divorced him seven years ago.

It's all a natural extension of those early camera ads – back when we were told no special moment had really happened unless we made it a "Kodak moment." Now every moment is special because it's a Nokia moment, or an Apple moment, or a Samsung moment. So no moment is special at all.

Yet we're only at the dawn of the photo age, as billions of cameras spread through every home and hut on the planet. Soon we will all wear computerized lapel-cams and hat-cams that take our pictures on their own, recording our lives every five minutes—or five seconds.

All we'll have to do is press the record 24/7 button, followed by the edit highlights feature that automatically creates a slide show of the day. Then we can all watch replays of it at home while we are being filmed watching it, so we have something else to watch next day.

But I suspect the more we shoot, the less there is to see.

Wrapping Rage

The most difficult part of buying modern products isn't getting them to work—which is hard enough. The real challenge is getting them out of the package.

Every object comes imprisoned in seven kilograms of indestructible plastic that encases everything from iPods to phone cards to individually wrapped screws. It's all part of our new plastic-wrapped world. Miniscule Nano music players come in boxes the size of TVs, while TVs come in boxes the size of pianos—and God knows what pianos come in.

It won't be long before cars come wrapped in packages the size of houses. Government regulations now legally require fifty times as much packaging as product—and it's causing 'wrapping rage'. Here are the worst packaging perils:

Small electronic items: Almost every device now comes inside plastic clamshell containers that are bulletproof, people-proof and welded shut at the seams. They repel scissors and steak knives as easily as toothpicks—and you must stab them repeatedly with an X-Acto knife until you slash through the package, or your sofa … or your abdomen.

It's best to read the fine print on the package carefully as it says something like: "*Wheretofore and heretofore and whereupon, whomsoever shall open said product does so with the knowledge that all knife wounds, screwdriver gashes, finger amputations, disembowellings, heart attacks and psychotic breakdowns are the sole responsibility of the package-opener—even if said device explodes while opening. It is advisable to have a package-handling lawyer present to inform you of your rights.*"

Eventually all gadgets will be required to come with mandatory how-to-open-the-container instructions, as well as a special kit for opening them—all wrapped in thick plastic.

Big box items: Giant TVs and air conditioners come packed in boxes stuffed with 127 giant pieces of styrofoam, molded so tightly to the product there's no room for your fingers. When you finally extricate the device after 40 minutes of sweating, you'll find dozens of plastic baggies at the bottom of the box—each containing individually-wrapped cables, remotes, batteries and other item—secured by plastic tie-ons that are knotted or welded shut.

Finally, there are thousands of tiny foam peanuts thrown in, just to waste more resources.

By the time you've unpacked it all, your living room reminds you of Christmas morning. Of course, you must recycle it all—but the city won't take large foam pieces. First, you must chop the foam into small bits, then saw the box into sections and fold and tie it all in a bundle. Before doing this, read the fine print again, as some brands may say: "Product warranty is null and void unless you have kept the box containing the original bar code serial number, along with all styrofoam peanuts—and we will count them."

Drugs: Pill and vitamin bottles are designed to keep out anyone under 4 or over 40. Once you remove the twist-top cap that does not twist, you must slash through the aluminum seal that doesn't have a tab to pull.

It's best to keep a steak knife by your night table, although you can also use your car keys. Afterwards, you must somehow fit your finger inside the bottle and wriggle it round till you remove the immense cotton ball that separates you from your four tiny pills. Now—where was my Valium? (Inside another sealed bottle).

Equally aggravating are gel caps embedded in aluminum foil cards that say "push to remove"—although that often causes several capsules to explode from the container. It's easier to just put the whole package in your mouth, chew it—and spit out the foil.

Other packaging challenges include potato chip bags so puffed up you can't grab the edges and you must rip them open with your teeth; pull-top soup cans where the loop snaps off and you suddenly need to find pliers; and CD wrappers sealed so tightly in cellophane that only a surgeon with a scalpel can remove it. This is the reason many people started buying all their music online—there's nothing to pry open.

How did we end up in this synthetic jungle, where an estimated 53 per cent of all products come buried in plastic that's smothering our products and our planet, filling landfills with stuff that will last for two million years? Partly it's because plastic is great for shipping and handling—and also keeps out shoplifters. This may be justifiable for a $500 Blackberry, but not for $2 batteries.

As our population gets older and feebler, the situation will only get worse. How many seniors already expire each week trying to break into their plastic-wrapped arugula? How many heart attacks do they suffer sawing through their new HDMI-cable containers?

There must be another way. Maybe we could have on-off switches on packages that deactivate to permit customer access once you leave the store and have proven you are not a shoplifter. Or maybe cashiers could automatically remove all packaging for us and recycle it.

We send people to the moon, insert microscopic cameras into scalpels for brain surgery and map the human genome. Surely we can find a way to break down the barrier between our products and us.

Let's send packaging packing—and unwrap the world.

Choose None of the Above

I was looking for a new television recently and the choices were awesome. I could get a plasma TV or an LCD TV with either HD or ED, or a CRT-based RPT. I could choose DLP rear projection or front projection, or abdominal C-section with dissection or even vivisection. The differences were so confusing I got a headache and decided I'd just keep my old TV for a few more years.

That's my usual response these days when I'm paralyzed by the staggering standard array of choices. Everywhere I turn, there is more choice to rejoice in. Do I want my jeans wide-cut, extra wide or baggy? Low-slung, high-strung, stressed, distressed, or stonewashed by Peruvian peasants using 1,000-year-old lava rocks and being paid fair trade salaries?

Milk used to be a simple item found on one small grocery shelf but now there's an entire wall of the stuff with options that are mind-numbing. You can choose skim milk, soy milk, rice milk or organic chai-flavored Vitamin D-fortified, lactose-free "Omega 3-DHA milk" enhanced with wild salmon.

No one drinks old milk milk anymore, which is now known as "fat-enhanced milk."

We are eons away from caveman days, when Dad would just say: "I'm thinking fresh-speared sabre tooth tiger for dinner, honey." Mom didn't ask whether he meant wild, farmed or free-range sabre tooth, or whether the tiger was grain-fed, grass-fed or organically grown in New Zealand with no antibiotics.

Dad didn't even have to worry about what kind of spear he was using: wood, metal, fiberglass, poly-composite or 100-per-cent organic recyclable material that causes no harm to the rainforest and is exempt from the federal government's online spear registry.

To make today's choices easier, many big supermarkets offer their own select choices, like President's Choice. But that still leaves 100 steak sauces to choose among—from *Memories of Shanghai* to

Amnesia in Malaysia to *What-Was-That-We-Ate in Kuwait.* Amidst the seven seas of choices, I always think I'm making the wrong decision. Is my Gold Air Miles bank card right for me, or should I switch to a new Enriched Plutonium card with built-in satellite reception and all my checks tracked by GPS?

Medicine also has dizzying new options. Doctors were once dictators who told you what to do as haughtily as five-star generals, but now they're democrats who ask you whether you'd like a heart bypass, or a stent or just a lot of Aspirin—so that whatever happens, you can only sue yourself. You can also decide where you want to visit a doctor, walk-in clinic, emergency ward, CLSC, community clinic or private clinic. Of course, no one can actually find a doctor to see these days, but you have a huge choice of where you can't see them.

The truth is we all need full-time assistants to make our choices for us, someone to cheerfully spend the day poring over our endless bank card and credit card offers, and comparing the daily chopped sirloin specials in the supermarket flyers. Nowadays, with apologies to the Rolling Stones, you *can* always get what you want—if you don't mind doing five days of Internet research and three days of comparative shopping.

No wonder many people simply can't keep up with the choices. Many poor souls suffer from choice burn-out, where they freeze up at even the simplest of decisions—like which one of a mere 178 cereals to buy. Or how to choose their new cellphone from among 163,000 models with 3.1 million features and 897 "personalized" phone plans offering a choice of 3,312 incoming pre-dawn weekday minutes, or 1,257 weekend twilight minutes, or 3,514 Summer Leap Year minutes with online photo development

Too much freedom can be a burden—and many of us secretly crave a dictator to tell us what to do, like our mothers once did. I wonder if a new generation raised in our multiple-choice whirl will eventually become so exhausted they crave the opposite? Will they decide that more choice just means more hassle and less time for life—that less choice can be more?

Will they demand new-style restaurants that tell them exactly what they must eat, or clothing brands that come in only one style, or arranged marriages with non-negotiable no-divorce-and-mandatory-two-kid clauses? Will they buy No Choice phones, drive No Choice cars and vote for a dictatorial No Choice Party that pledges to outlaw every last confusing decision?

Will they choose not to choose? I can see the future—a McDictator chain, or a Burger Boss where a confident waiter makes all your decisions. "Good evening, sir. You'll be having the ribs to-night while your wife will be getting the chicken Caesar. You'll both be having the salad with Italian dressing, low-cal by the look of you. Now relax. I'll be back in a minute to tell you what you're drinking. And if you want anything else, I'll let you know."

PLEASE CHOOSE YOUR OWN ENDING FOR THIS STORY:

1. Suddenly, everyone was hit by a train.

2. Sorry Josh, I'm too busy. You choose the ending and I'll tell you whether it's any good.

3. Uh, what were those choices again?

Read This While Driving

You're probably doing something else while you read this story, like riding the subway, or biking on a machine at your health club, or sitting in your car and reading the funny parts aloud to your husband. "Listen Henry! He says I'm reading this story to you while we're driving. That's funny! *Ohmigod!! ... Lookout-for-the-fire-hydrannntttt!*"

In our modern multi-tasking world who has time to simply read a story when you could also be baking a cake and doing a crossword puzzle? Doing just one thing is so ... yesterday.

OK, OK, people have always done two things at once, but they did simpler things—like walking and chewing gum. Or smoking and coughing. Or when feeling risqué, tapping their fingers on the steering wheel while listening to the car radio.

But then in the '80s we started to juggle more complex tasks. First, we learned how to eat and walk, then jog and listen to the Walkman, then flip through channels with a remote so we could watch 14 programs simultaneously. Now new combinations are invented every day by the World Multi-Task task force.

I know many people who love to watch TV and listen to the radio at the same time, apparently using each ear for a different task. Others floss their teeth in the car, while they drive with their knees. In fact, while I write this, I'm talking on the phone and dancing the rhumba.

More than 50 per cent of our meals are now eaten in front of the TV, multi-tasking headquarters for modern teens. They do their homework while streaming music videos while texting their friends while Skyping, while channel-surfing during commercials. And if you criticize them they say:

"Da-aad, I can't possibly concentrate on my homework unless I'm doing three other things. It's so *Neanderthal* to use your whole brain for just one thing."

Most of my phone calls nowadays are from friends who are doing something else while talking to me on their cell, whether they're skiing, cycling, picking up their dry cleaning or shopping for dinner. "Hey, Josh! How are you? ... Sorry—can you hang on while I order? ... Gimme two pounds of smoked meat, medium, with a side of coleslaw. No, not creamy! ... the good stuff! So hey!—Josh—how *ARE* you?"

Even when people are with me they're busy glancing at their phone screens where more interesting things than me are obviously happening. Who knows what I'm competing with: the latest news flash about Gadhafi's death, the Greek Euro crisis, the quarter-hourly local weather update—or just another Twitter from their kids saying "mlkshkes at DQ mum—mmmm."

It's all a symptom of our inattentive society. You're probably thinking of jumping ahead now to the next story about coffee shops—but don't. I still need your full partial attention. Even when we're alone working, the ping of email keeps tempting us, breaking our concentration with its siren call. In fact, I just heard mine so pardon me while I check it...

OK—I'm back! It was just a U.K. Lottery company offering me another chance to win 22 million euros. I hope I win, while there's still a Euro.

Now what was I saying? Oh yeah—the big question is: How much can our attention spans shrink? Experts warn we are already incapable of finishing weighty novels like *War and Peace*. In fact, Tolstoy probably couldn't have finished writing it if he'd had to answer all his email.

What we demand of ourselves we also demand of our gadgets, which multiply our multi-tasking ability. It's not enough to be a music player anymore; it has to be a pedometer/clock/satellite radio/music player that gives the weather and the barometric pressure on seven continents. Simple printers are passé—they must be printer-scanner-fax-machines that also develop photos.

No one wants a simple cellphone nowadays —it has to be a GPS camera-phone, with a telescopic zoom lens that can see the Mars

Rover. It must also take videos and stream TV channels, so you can film yourself watching *Survivor* while you drive to the cottage eating from your bucket of KFC chicken. But don't be surprised if you mistakenly bring the drumstick to your ear and find yourself chewing on the phone.

In her book *Distracted*, author Maggie Jackson warns of the shallow modern attention span she calls "Mcthinking." She says it's "eroding our capacity for deep, sustained, perceptive attention and stunting society's …"

Uh … whatever.

The Coff-E-Shop

I have seen the future and it's a coffee shop. Every Second Cup or Starbucks I step into is packed with people sitting at their laptops, busily typing away.

They're finishing novels and term papers, writing emails and reading e-newspapers, doing their banking, composing music or just chatting online to other people in other coffee shops in other cities, or countries or coffee galaxies. There are more people on computers in coffee shops on our planet than there are people drinking coffee.

I thought the coffee shop craze was ending when Starbucks fever started fading a couple of years ago. But they were just the advance guard of a brave new coffee shop world. Even McDonald's now serves espressos and frappa-zappa-cappuccino-style drinks, served by coffee "baristas," while staid old Tim Horton's is in a foam over its new lattes.

Yet for most customers, the coffee isn't really why they're there—it's just an excuse to sit and use the Wifi, surrounded by other humans. These Internet speakeasies shouldn't even be called coffee shops—they're really coff-E-shops.

Partly, they're driven by student power. When I was in college we hung out in libraries to study, but who needs those anymore? Today's students have more books available on their laptops than I did in the whole McGill Library—and you don't have to whisper to use them. So many students study in coffee shops that eventually Java U will become a real university, with degree-granting powers that permit it to award diligent customers a Master of Cappuccino in History, or a Doctor of Latin Latte.

Yet while students drive the success of Starbucks, they're small bucks compared to what's coming. We live in a world where fewer and fewer people work in offices and more and more have the lonely freedom to work at home. Many people aren't cut out for their own lone company and miss their old water cooler camaraderie, so they take their laptops somewhere they can find coffee camaraderie, while socializing in cyberspace.

For all you know I'm writing this story from a coffee shop, and for all I know you're reading it in one.

As ever more jobs are outsourced to home workers I suspect office-nostalgic workers will start to congregate together in their own chosen coffee shops. Eventually, we may see giant coffee-drinking factories with separate work alcoves rented out to each office-deprived group, like writers, architects and broke stockbrokers.

Meanwhile, as the recession leaves more people unemployed, they're coming to coffee houses too, to search the Internet job ads, surrounded by other people competing for the same jobs. More and more people are doing their shopping online too—buying records, books and clothes on the Net—and many do this in coffee houses too, abandoning crowded stores for crowded cafés.

It won't be long before stores are virtually empty because we're all shopping virtually. There will be no more supermarkets—just online grocery shopping done in coffee shops, where you'll squeeze the Internet tomato before it's delivered. Or smell the virtual coffee.

As coffee houses become powerhouses, no one will be left in offices—we'll become a nation of coffee shop patrons (and waiters) eager for human company. By then, we will all work at coff-E shops, e-groceries, e-burger joints, e-universities and even e-barbershops. Don't ask me how—but there will be e-barbers, as well as e-dentists and e-heart-surgeons, all working out of coff-E-shops.

This rebirth of the coffee house makes perfect sense in our techno-revolutionary era. In the 1700s, the new European coffee houses were where intellectuals like Voltaire and Rousseau gathered to debate the ideas that set off the Enlightenment. If they hadn't had coffee houses where they could stay up all night and argue, there might never have been a French Revolution. We'd all still be serfs instead of surfing the Web.

So the coming coffee shop revolution may only be a re-run of the past. But instead of a French Revolution there will be an e-revolution. And instead of meeting for a coffee we will just meet for an E.

A Post-Emily Post Guide to Etiquette

I recently saw a movie the guy beside me obviously didn't like—because he was busy organizing his emails. Throughout the film, he tapped away on his phone, reading and deleting mail, and perhaps checking his stocks. Maybe he was also reading reviews of other movies in the same theater he could go to instead.

All I know is that his lit-up screen distracted me from watching the film, because it's hard to ignore one screen and watch another. Besides, I kept looking at his screen to see if any of the messages were for me.

The amazing thing is that it never occurred to him he might be annoying his neighbors. Like many people, he has no clue about the rules of modern etiquette—because there aren't any. It's time for a guide to modern manners, a 21st-century post-Emily Post advice manual that tells us how to behave in public. In Miss Post's absence let me offer Mister Josh's Short Guide to Modern Etiquette. And if you don't like my suggestions, just shove off, okay pal?

Phone Etiquette: Cellphones should not be confused with megaphones. Do not speak into them as if addressing a stadium of anti-war protesters. It's difficult to grasp, but your conversation about your daughter's horse show is not compelling to everyone—some of us are self-centered egomaniacs who just don't care that she won the silver medal for dressage.

When using your cell, it's best to assume people nearby don't want to hear your conversation. Speak as if you're having a personal conversation between two people—not like you're onstage in Hamlet. Think cellphone, not yellphone.

Fortunately phones ringing in movies have now become quite rare as everyone knows this is the worst social mistake on the planet. Audience reactions can become so violent, I sometimes feel bad for the person whose phone is ringing. If you get stuck in this situation, it's advisable not to answer your phone at all—just look around indignantly like everyone else, until the ringing stops.

Email Etiquette is also evolving. For instance, some occasional spelling mistakes are fine, bt nt in evy wrd becse thts annoying nd hrd to red.

CAPITAL LETTERS ARE NOT TO BE OVERUSED. IT'S LIKE SHOUTING—UNLESS YOU ARE SENDING NIGERIAN EMAIL, WHERE THIS IS THE PROPER STYLE.

It's okay to check your mail while walking or jogging, but not while conversing with someone, or driving, or at symphonies, funerals, operas or houses of worship. It's okay to hire someone by email, but don't use it to fire them. Lately I'm also getting birth, death and wedding announcements by email. It won't be long before you'll be able to split up with your spouse by sending them a public email saying: "I divorce thee," three times.

Airplane Etiquette is especially awkward nowadays, because you and your seatmate are sharing a seat that's only big enough for one. Surprisingly, just because you weigh three times as much as your neighbor doesn't mean you get three times the room.

The border between seats officially starts at the armrest, which is exactly big enough for half an arm per person. The line extends right up to the airplane roof, which means you shouldn't fall asleep with your head resting on your seatmate's shoulder, or lap.

It's fine to use a computer, but your screen width should not exceed your seat width. When placing your seat in the recline position, remember to do so gently, because you may be crushing the person behind you to death. The one good thing about modern flights is you don't have to worry about spilling food on your neighbor anymore—because there isn't any food.

Queue Etiquette: When standing in line always face forward, even if the view is dull. Facing backwards isn't viewed well especially by the person you're staring at.

In North America, never stand too close to the person ahead of you or they'll think you're trying to steal their wallet, or kiss them on the neck. However in India, China or Poland it's crucial to cram together like lemmings, in order to keep your place. Lean back to stretch and you'll never un-stretch, because five families will squeeze into the gap where your chest was.

Bus Seat Etiquette: Giving your seat up to an elderly person is tricky today because many of them don't consider themselves old. They may just feel you are announcing to the whole bus that THIS PERSON IS AN OLD PERSON! In some U.S. states they might even bring a suit against you alleging age discrimination.

Study the aging person carefully and ask yourself how they see themselves. If they're wearing micro jogging shorts or a Boston Marathon nose ring, do not offer your seat. If they're carrying a cane and five shopping bags, give it a try.

If they're bald with a grey beard, that's me—and I like standing, punk!

6

Planet Mirth

Save the Seven Billion

[November 2, 2011]

Hi everyone—all seven billion of you!
It's me, Josh, world citizen Number 2,502,297,825. At least that's the number calculated for me by a new BBC website where they ask your date of birth, then tell you what number person you were on the planet the day you were born.

I was the 2,502,29,825th person alive on Earth back then—a far cry from today's population which reportedly hit seven billion a couple of nights ago on Halloween night. I don't want to get nostalgic, but life was a lot more intimate on Earth back when there were just 2.5 billion of us.

Back then, we all knew each other's names—and remembered each other's birthdays and four-digit phone numbers. But today, with seven billion of us, who can keep up? In fact, when I checked the latest "live" online world population count ten minutes ago, it was already up to 7,000,077,280. And as I write this sentence, it's just jumped again—to 7,000,100,013.

No wonder I barely know any of you anymore, or see you on the street. And I've been looking. I've been to China and India recently, where I saw lots of people—but seven billion? No way. Where are you all hiding? Experts say it's because we humans don't actually take up much room—standing shoulder to shoulder we could all squeeze into the city of Los Angeles. Or onto 2.5 Montreal Islands.

It's not us that takes up space. It's our stuff—seven billion of us wanting seven billion houses, 14 billion cellphones and 21 billion TVs. Not to mention no end of golf courses, swimming pools, SUVs, expressways, espressos, drive-ins, Big Macs, Whoppers and supersized 80-ounce Cokes.

Frankly, seven billion is too big a number to envision. I can imagine 20,000 people watching a hockey game, or conceivably even a million-person march. But 7 billion of anything is hard to grasp—it takes your breath away.

For instance, seven billion seconds ago, the year was 1789, and George Washington was U.S. president.

If you went seven billion kilometers into space in a rocket, you'd get slightly past the space rock formerly known as Pluto. Then again, seven billion stars are just a drop in the bucket compared to what scientists think are out there. So next time you look up at the sky and say: "Wow, there must be a billion stars," you're way off. According to astronomers, the correct statement is: "Wow, there must be a trillion billion stars out there."

How about seven-billion dollars? According to a U.S. study, $7 billion is the total income of 4,200 men or 5,300 women over their entire lifetimes. It's also what Facebook founder Mark Zuckerberg had in the bank last time I checked. Maybe all those young protesters ought to "Occupy Facebook!" instead of joining it.

The average human arm span is about five feet. So if all seven billion of us held out our arms and linked hands, we could circle the globe about 268 times. That'd be a nice way to celebrate the seven billionth person in the human family.

The bad news is that if every one of us had a car we would have seven billion vehicles—and total planetary gridlock. But seven billion votes would be great for democracy—I suspect most people would just vote for more food, more water and more fuel, because almost half the planet doesn't have enough.

Finally, if every one of us seven billion humans was a grain of sand we could fill about 63 buckets. But if we poured that on the shoreline during high tide, it would all wash away in seconds—a reminder of how fragile seven billion of anything really is.

Fortunately there's a simpler way to imagine all seven billion of us. The population of my home province, Quebec is some seven million plus—so seven billion people is just 1,000 Quebecs. Now that sounds a lot more manageable, doesn't it—practically like a neighborhood.

All we need is 1,000 premiers to run things and enough money to rebuild 1,000 Champlain Bridges and fix 1,000 billion potholes, which isn't as many as stars, but close.

In fact, back when there were only six million Quebecers, there was a great beer ad that said: *On est six millions, faut se parler.* Maybe an updated English translation would be a good slogan for the world, too: "We're seven billion—let's talk."

The time is right. Almost three-quarters of the world is reported to have a cellphone and soon the rest will too—so at last we can all call each other up and have a friendly chat.

Forget the G8, or the G20. It's time for the G7 billion.

It's Clonely You

OK, enough cloning around. In the last week, I've heard enough about the Raelians and their aliens to last me five cloned lifetimes.

If these cult members ever actually prove they've cloned a baby girl named Eve, we'll never hear the end of it. They'll be announcing more clones every month, with names like Adam, Noah, Cain, Job, Jesus, Mary, Moses and Obadiah.

And that's just the start. According to the group's leaders, we will all be able to create baby clones of ourselves as we get older, to make sure our genes live forever after we're gone. But please don't tell that to Stephen Harper: we'll never get rid of him.

Frankly, the whole idea sounds like a nightmare. Who wants to have another me wandering around my house, making things twice as messy as they already are? Who needs someone else losing the remote, forgetting where the car is parked, or getting locked out of the house?

One of me is enough, thanks. That's why most of us marry people who aren't like us. We're looking for some variety while cloning is the opposite—and would make for a duller world. Even if I died, I'm not sure my family would want me replaced with exactly the same model of Josh—they'd probably prefer an upgrade, a Josh who could program the TiVo machine, install the air-conditioner and read a road map when we're on holidays.

But cloning isn't about what others want. It's about "me." It's the natural step in a narcissistic world, where everyone's obsessed with their own future and their own immortality. In fact, if cloning ever becomes the rage, we won't be hearing about the ME generation anymore—we'll be hearing about the "me and me" generation.

I can already imagine the ad at the Raelian laboratory, where they produce their human duplicates. "WHY BE ALONE? GET A CLONE!" Pretty soon we'll be living in a world full of clone wolves, all wandering around in identical pairs.

Our cultural life will be boring too. Entertainment will decline once clones get in on the act, and movie producers start getting rid of big, expensive casts. The big kids' film of the future will be called *Home Aclone,* starring Macaulay Culkin and Macaulay Culkin. The Simpsons will all be named Bart. The Clone Rangers will dump Tonto in the remake.

Music will follow with re-makes of great old songs, like "Only the Clonely," while the tabloid press will have endless stories like: "Man Disowned by Own Clone."

OK, enough cloning around. This is a serious issue we will probably have to face soon or later. The fact is that one reason evolution works so well is that it adds the unknown to our future, it lets us produce children who aren't quite like us or our mates—just an unpredictable mix.

However, with cloning we will all eventually have the same allergies, opinions and tastes. And it won't be long before we start feeling "clonely," the new word we'll need to describe the sensation that you can't get away from yourself.

But even that's not the end of it. It's only a matter of time before two clones announce they want to get married in a same-sex ceremony—and then imagine the issues it will raise.

Marrying yourself would obviously have some advantages. You could share the same wardrobe, and you'd never argue over what to watch on TV; but on the down side, you'd always be grabbing the same section of the paper. And you'd open a bottomless can of worms.

Can you have children with your clone? And if you do, are you the real parents, or are your parents who cloned you? Or your grandparents who cloned them? The whole thing is like living in a house of mirrors.

To tell the truth I get a headache just thinking about it—but that's still better than the two headaches I'll have when I'm cloned. No thanks, Raelians, I won't be showing up at your lab.

To borrow from the immortal Greta Garbo: "I don't vant to be aclone."

Alien Nation

Single, lonely, crowded planet seeks friendly, compatible alien planet for meaningful long-distance relationship that's out of this world. Would prefer older, mature, more peaceful planet than our own.

Aliens—they're everywhere you turn.

Ten years ago, aliens were something hermits in Texas saw filing into a UFO in their backyard, or that made *National Enquirer* headlines—like "Michael Jackson Fathers Alien's Love Child."

But now the people talking about aliens are highly respectable scientists like Stephen Hawking—and they seem convinced we'll find company in our cosmos in the next 30 years. Or 300. Or 3,000.

There are also major Hollywood films about aliens—from the story of the "secret" Apollo 18 mission (whose astronauts were "murdered by aliens"), to *Cowboys and Aliens* with Harrison Ford. There are serious TV science specials about aliens, such as *Message from Space* and *The Great Extraterrestrial Debate*.

Behind our growing alien obsession is the fact astronomers are suddenly discovering several planets a minute, using humongous new telescopes that see many solar systems past ours. They say they've detected billions of distant planets—and it's only a matter of time before they spot one with an alien on it looking back at us through a bigger telescope.

All this brings up that age-old question: What would aliens look like? Planet Hollywood has provided our image of them since we were kids—from creepy little green men to lovable bug-eyed ETs. But now scientists are drawing their own portraits of what to expect based on the laws of science.

England's National Space Centre planetarium has even come up with a best guesstimate of what an alien would look like. They say it would probably be bigger than a rat—since rats have small brains and intelligent life would need a bigger brain. But it shouldn't be much bigger than an elephant because "that would make it hard to stand without toppling over."

The scientists' model alien has two eyes just like us, because most planets get starlight—and everything on Earth living in light has eyes. Eleven eyes could work too, say scientists but that seems unlikely since it would take up lots of brain power—with little added advantage apart from making sure no one could sneak up behind you and say "Boo!"

Either way, if they're a highly evolutionarily-advanced species, I suspect the aliens will have better eyesight than us so they can read the tiny print on airline ads, credit card contracts, pill bottles, ingredient lists—and even the White Pages.

They will probably also have at least a dozen hands to handle all the gadgets even we backwards humans have invented. That way they could drive a flying saucer while making intergalactic cellphone calls, sending text messages at the speed of light, eating space junk food and flossing their 121 teeth.

Scientists assume that aliens would be way more intelligent than us since we Homo sapiens are just babes on the galactic block—less than 200,000 years old in a universe that may be 15 billion years old. So we should expect any extraterrestrials to be at least a million years old and have discovered a cure for wrinkles.

Frankly, it might be better if aliens are more technologically backward than us so we can sell them our crappy old DOS-based computers and 8-track tapes at inflated prices—maybe even trade one of their planet's continents for some beads and firewater. It might be safer for us humans if they were vegetarians too, so in case of disputes we won't remind them of lunch.

Other questions come to mind: Will they be ecologically advanced, with spacecraft that resemble a giant Prius run on "dilithium crystals" as in Star Trek? Or will they have a huge, gas-belching flying saucer surrounded by a shroud of pollution—an airborne version of a '56 Chevy, because gas came back into fashion in their solar system after they discovered 1,000 all-oil planets?

Most importantly, would they welcome us humans with warm

open arms, or tentacles, or whatever? Would they treat us like cosmic comrades, precious friends who share a vast, empty, meaningless universe—or could they treat us like we treated the Native Peoples?

The worst-case scenario is probably that they are too much like us—as greedy violent and ready to exploit resources and other species as we human beings. Maybe it's better if we're all alone in the cosmos—and there's nothing else like us out there in space, but space.

The fact is, human beings can be alienating.

Al Jesteera Covers the Student Strike

JUNE 2012: Montreal has suddenly become a global hotspot as our student strike makes news in almost one hundred countries and over three thousand foreign news reports.

What are they all saying about us? I've just learned that a reporter for a small Middle Eastern paper called *Al Jesteera* has been in Montreal, investigating the "student revolution."

I've obtained his first report. An English translation follows:

Greetings my revolutionary brothers! I am thrilled to be in Montreal, latest stop in the global rebellion against dictatorship.

First came the Tunisian, Egyptian and Libyan Awakenings—and now the Great Quebec Awakening, where revolutionary students have massed to overthrow the brutal Liberal government and their strongman Charest.

As a specialist covering revolutions from Afghanistan to Zagreb, I arrived with my standard survival gear: bulletproof vest, bottled water ("Clearly Jordanian") and freeze-dried falafel. Before arriving today, I read numerous international news reports about Montreal, a city reportedly in chaos from protests against Bill 78—a repressive new anti-demonstration law that apparently makes the Mullahs of Iran seem like Democrats.

Now—I'm off to the streets to see the Revolution in action. My eyewitness account follows:

JUNE 24: How exciting! The very day I arrived, the city was occupied by armies of rebel protesters who marched through the streets flying Quebec flags in honor of "St. Jean" —obviously some past revolutionary hero. Many in the crowd beat pots and pans, perhaps in reference to the tin-pot dictator Jean Charest. Or maybe it was just the hungry demanding food, I am unsure.

One young protester generously offered me his casseroles to beat but I confess I was unable to do it—back home I have only one pot and it is very precious.

JUNE 28: Today vast throngs converged downtown to see freedom-fighting artists at giant gatherings in the Quartier des Spectacles—Montreal's Tahrir Square. This took great courage since the area was cordoned off by plainclothes secret police in T-shirts bearing the strange English word "Jazzfest."

Given how people obeyed them, these jazz paramilitaries are as fearsome as were Mubarak's secret police, They searched every knapsack, confiscating liquor like Iran's Revolutionary Guard—but then inexplicably sold their own liquor inside the jazz area. Truly, the ways of the West are mysterious to me.

At night great masses joined the jazz uprising—setting up temporary stages where they played revolutionary music. Over 100,000 watched rebel leader Rufus Wainwright sing freedom hymns—in the largest crush of humanity I have seen since the fall of the Berlin Wall.

Amidst the chaos I lost my water bottle and falafel rations. For nourishment I purchased something called *poutine*—the French spelling of Putin—evidently some tribute to Russia's Vladimir Poutine, The mood seemed festive, but I kept on my bulletproof vest. I remember the first innocent days of Tahrir Square.

That night, awake in my hotel, I heard the sound of loud artillery explosions. Looking out, I saw the sky over the river lit up by apparent tracer fire—all too familiar from my days covering Syria. The Quebec army was obviously warning the rebels to abandon the "jazzfest" area. Yet the crowds in the streets didn't panic—they just gazed at the illuminated sky in awe, as innocently as if they were watching fireworks.

JUNE 29: I did not leave my hotel bed all day as I was unwell. The Russian *poutine* did not agree with me.

JULY 1: Tension had mounted during my absence. Downtown streets were clogged with small trucks loaded with refugees apparently fleeing the city. Hundreds of thousands were abandoning their homes in one of the largest exoduses since the Partition of India.

Many desperate souls dragged refrigerators and stoves down the stairs. I asked one man carrying a sofa what was happening—and he said ominously it was "Moving Day." This was some code I didn't understand—so I asked where he was being relocated:

"To N.D.G.," he said. Could this be an acronym for the "National Detention Gulag"?

JULY 9: Jazzfest ended days ago but mass gatherings continue downtown. Today tens of thousands of African-Quebecers marched to demand their rights. Many dressed in Caribbean garb and danced while carrying mysterious signs saying "Carifiesta."

I joined in—and it was more fun than Arab Spring.

I am told another protest called Nuits d'Afriques begins now, then a nihilist gathering that grimly calls itself The Comedy Festival. What a strange place this city is, where warring parties dance together instead of fight—bathed in music, not blood. I have never seen so many nationalities co-exist this happily, even in the UN assembly. Yet we never hear about this in world press coverage of the "student crisis".

Brothers! The "Montreal situation" is obviously more complex than we were led to believe. In fact, I am taking up temporary residency here in Montreal. It is far more safe and festive than any war zone—or peace zone—I have visited. If this is Montreal during its "troubles", imagine what it is like at peace.

P.S. I am even learning to like *poutine.*

Blame the Babylonians

[January 14, 2012]

We're two weeks days into 2012 and I'm still keeping up with my New Year's resolutions—because my only resolution was to have no resolutions.

All over the world millions of people have made ambitious promises, such as: "I will stop smoking, drinking, eating meat and spending money," or "I will begin a daily three-hour exercise regime to lose 100 pounds, although I only weigh 150."

Yet a quarter of these people have already given up—and the rest will follow in the next two months. Last week they went to the gym five times, while eating one meal a day. This week they'll only go to the gym twice and by late February they won't be going at all, but will be eating five times a day to console themselves. They will be filled with safe-hatred and muttering to themselves: "I'm a useless ball of lard that can't even keep the simplest promise."

Yet it wasn't simple at all—it was one of the hardest promises of their lives. That's because they foolishly made their New Year's resolutions on New Year's Day—the worst possible time of year to keep any resolution in Canada.

It is the dead of winter, when we face three, long, cold months that require all our resolve to survive—without adding extra resolutions. It is exactly when we are most likely to gain weight, because in winter we crave heavy, fat food to stay alive. Why fight millennia of evolution—do bears prepare for hibernation with a diet?

It's also the hardest time of year to exercise, because you can't go anywhere without shoveling out the car, by which time you're too exhausted to go anywhere at all, let alone exercise. That's why countless new health clubs are created in December, before the Great New Year's Rush, so they can close in mid-February, when there are no members left to notice.

Winter is the hardest time of year to give up anything. Swearing off liquor is easy in July when you're sitting on your balcony sipping icy fruit smoothies—but winter is exactly when you need a stiff drink, or three. Quitting smoking is also a fabulous idea but not in January. Winter makes even me want to light up—and I've never smoked.

So why do we do it? Whose idea was it to make our resolutions precisely when we can't keep them?

Blame it on the ancient Babylonians who traditionally started each year by promising to bring back any farm equipment they'd borrowed. In fact they didn't keep their promises any better than we do and the stuff piled up in their fields while they borrowed more scythes, oxen, slaves and water wheels.

The ancient Romans were also big on resolutions. They typically resolved to eat fewer nineteen-course meals, while spending less time in the vomitorium and more at aerobic activities—like pillaging, crucifying and orgies. But by late February most of them were back in the vomitorium and had dropped their memberships in the Young Mens' Gladiatorial Association (YMGA).

It's time we put an end to this ancient, self-hating New Year's custom. Next year we must all resolve to delay our resolutions to a date when we have some hope of keeping them. Let's choose our own personal New Year's, like the Jewish New Year in September, which gives us three months to practice our resolutions before winter sets in.

How about the Muslim New Year in July, an excellent time to curtail eating, or try fasting? You can also pick Canada Day, or April Fool's Day, or whatever date suits your resolve. But if you do insist on sticking with our ridiculous mid-winter New Year's habit, at least make realistic resolutions you have some hope of keeping. Here are some suggestions:

I resolve not to weigh that much more at the end of winter than at the start. I resolve to eat thick stews and not to obsess over calories because I need them to survive. I acknowledge that iceberg lettuce is not a winter food.

I resolve not to have more than three drinks a day, unless it is a special occasion. I resolve not to take up smoking for the first time, or start using crack cocaine, or heroin, or more serious drugs. If I finish winter in no worse shape than I started, I shall be proud.

If all else fails, I absolutely and solemnly resolve to bring back any farm equipment I have borrowed in the last year.

Hans Up

[July 2005]

Something's rotten in the state of Denmark-Canada relations. The two countries are suddenly facing off over who owns Hans Island, a desolate speck of frozen rock somewhere in the Canadian—or Danish—Arctic.

Canada has announced it has sovereignty over this deserted oversized boulder, but Denmark has angrily warned Canada to keep its hands off Hans. Now the war of words is heating up faster than our Arctic's icebergs.

There are rumors Denmark may seize the island by force and rename it Hans Christian Andersen, and reports that Canada will round up all Great Danes living in our country and place them in internment kennels. Could we be heading for war between two cold and dull nations, one known for Hamlet, the other for hockey?

Militarily, the two sides are evenly matched. Canada's navy has four second-hand submarines, while the Danes have four supersize herrings. Each country boasts soldiers trained as UN blue helmets, but the Danes also have a blue cheese battalion. Both countries have huge divisions of think tanks, though Denmark's reportedly suffer from "Hamlet syndrome"—which makes for lots of indecision. "To be or not be—in Hans—that is the question."

My sources tell me young Canadian sharpshooters are already being handpicked for for a possible large snowball fight with the Danes—where the last person standing would win, Hans down. Other creative ways of settling the dispute under consideration are a dogsled race, a chess match, or a walrus throw.

Canada may also flex its economic muscle. For instance, we could launch a boycott of Danish modern furniture, though it's probably all made by workers in China. We could also impose a travel ban on Canadian tourists going to Denmark and get 100-per-cent compliance, since no Canadian tourists go to Denmark anyway.

However, Ottawa fears that Denmark might retaliate by withdrawing Canada's right to refer to soggy pastries as "Danish." Instead, we would have to call them "sticky buns." In fact, the Danes have long objected to this misuse of their national name. In Denmark, soggy pastries are always referred to as "Canadians."

Ultimately, what's beneath the tiff? Some officials say we're asserting our rights to claim future Arctic oil. But I hear the government is just eager for a small international spat to distract Canadians from our domestic problems. My sources tell me Canada's defense minister has been secretly looking for a small, safe country to take on.

Australia, Jamaica and Cuba were all deemed "too tough to mess with," as were 189 of the world's 193 countries. The choice eventually came down to Fiji, San Marino, Tonga and Denmark's Hans Island—and the last is the only place our 40-year-old helicopters can reach.

The government figures the worst-case scenario is that Denmark will win and occupy Canada—but the two countries are so similar, Canadians won't know the difference, apart from having to learn Danish. The bigger danger is that Canada might win and have to annex Denmark. Then we'd spend decades hearing the Danes go on about how they want to separate while keeping Medicare and the Canadian dollar. The mere thought is enough to make most of us throw up our Hans.

Armchair Protester

[2004]

I've recently become an armchair revolutionary. I attend street demonstrations every night, surrounded by people shouting "Down with the Tyrant!" I stand united with a million brave protesters—well, actually I sit, in the comfort of my La-Z-Boy.

I get enraged when dictators send troops to shoot my fellow global citizens and I demand justice for them. Then I switch channels to see what coverage is like on other networks. I am a couch-potato protester, channel-surfing my way through the revolutions in the Middle East.

I never saw it coming. Only months ago I couldn't find Yemen on the map but now I know the president's name (Ali Abdullah Saleh), the capital city (Sanaa) and the international dialing code (967). I've learned to pronounce Bahrain correctly with a slight gargle on the R. I know the names of more Egyptian opposition leaders than I do cabinet ministers in our Conservative government.

I didn't plan to become a Mideast junkie—but every time I start watching my favorite TV shows I get antsy. In minutes I find myself clicking to the latest protest coverage and next thing I know I'm hooked on revolution again.

Nothing on TV can match it. The "revolution" has it all—hope, fear, dread, drama, idealism, passion. The villains are as evil and weird as anything in the movies. Who could make up the murderous Colonel Gadaffi, a mad psychopathic mobster who'd have been comic if he wasn't ready to kill his entire country for the sake of his country?

Or Hosni Mubarak, the deposed strongman who made off with more money than Bernie Madoff. Or all the other oily members of the Arab Dictator-for-Life Club. There are wonderful heroes, too, like the young Google exec who launched Egypt's virtual revolution, then casually refused a leadership role to go back to his Googling job.

It's not easy being a TV revolutionary. At 9 p.m. I go to BBC for the latest level-headed revolution news. At 9:07 I switch to CNN for emotional eyewitness accounts and overheated anchors shouting things like "Gaddafi is even crazier than Mubarak—he's seriously unhinged."

Minutes later I flip to Aljazeera for an Arab perspective and then to CBC for the Canadian perspective—with official reaction from someone like the Minister of Agriculture, or the Minister of State for Sports. Whatever you're watching, the remarkable thing is that you are witnessing history in the making, as if you'd watched the 1917 Russian Revolution on live TV.

"Excuse me, Mr. Lenin! ... Mr. Lenin! I'm Anderson Cooper from CNN. Could I get a few words with you about this so-called revolution of yours? By the way, Mr. Lenin, I loved your song 'Give Peace a Chance.'"

Imagine seeing the French Revolution, with a live media scrum of Marie Antoinette: "Your Highness—many peasants are upset about the alleged remark you made about 'eating cake'. Would you like to clarify that, or take this chance to apologize to our viewers now?" If she had, she might have kept her head.

Despite my revolutionary enthusiasm I have fears too. I know the young Arab Internet generation is leading this revolution, but will it remain that way? Will elections eventually bring a new democracy or a religious government by Big Brotherhood? Where will the revolution spread next—Syria? Iran? Will protesters seize Dubai's giant indoor ski hill and demand ski passes for the masses?

Despite my fears I remain a dedicated armchair revolutionary, because the protesters on my screen are remarkably brave and dignified and deserve my support. They want what we take for granted: justice, a decent economy, freedom of speech and the right to a 64-inch flat-screen plasma TV.

Young Arabs have even given new dignity to Facebook and Twitter as the usual "c u at Strbks at 5 for a soy latte" becomes "cu at the demo at 6. Bring masks and vinegar 4 tear gas."

Speaking of demonstrations I have one to attend. It's 5 p.m.

and crowds are massing for protests in Tripoli—or was it Doba? Or Cairo? They're armed with placards, sticks and stones—and I am armed, too, my finger on the clicker.

The Santa clause

From Santa's Workshop, N.P.

Hello children!
Tonight is Christmas Eve and I'm chilling out, here at the North Pole, before starting my deliveries.

My apologies—you send me letters every Christmas but I haven't written back in years. My Christmas has gotten crazily busy, what with globalization and kids everywhere wanting everything. And not just kids. I get letters from adults wanting jobs, companies wanting endorsements, politicians seeking re-election and Russian XXX girls wanting to marry "a portly-looking older gentleman from a northern climate."

We've had a couple of exhausting years here at Santa's Workshop since we laid off half our elves during the 2008 recession. Things are picking up but the Christmas toy business has definitely changed. No one wants regular stuff like teddy bears anymore—they want iPhones, iPads, iPods, iPets and other iStuff. It's all about "I" today —sometimes I wish more kids asked for a "we" game instead of a Wii game, or an Us-box instead of an X-box.

It's not easy keeping up with new toy technology—from "e-poker for kids" to the latest "Barbie-in-Drag" app. We've recently started outsourcing to Chinese elves but we've had to recall some gifts, like a Santa doll with lead paint and an asbestos beard that was seized by Environment Canada.

There are other modern challenges. I can't deliver holly anymore because some children are allergic to it, or hand out ice cream bars because other kids are lactose-intolerant, or give kids chocolate reindeer because of possible peanut contamination. Even candy canes are frowned on by parents who call them "sugar sticks."

We have labor problems too. Rudolph was stopped again for drunken sleighing last Christmas by the police just because he has a red nose. Thank goodness he passed his Breathalyzer test, but Blitzen was one eggnog over the limit and his flying permit was suspended until summer.

Now a new Reindeer Rights group is claiming our sleighs work illegal all-night shifts during Christmas and they're calling Santa's Workshop "Santa's Sweatshop." They want me to switch to robot reindeer but Prancer and Dancer are indignant and say we're exempt from the labor code under the Santa clause.

There are border hassles too, when crossing from Canada into U.S. air space. I did a test run from Montreal to Burlington last month and the U.S. security guard searched my beard, then groped my stomach for so long I thought he wanted to jingle my bells.

There are even political battles. Everyone suddenly wants a piece of the North Pole after millennia of treating it like a block of ice. Several countries are lobbying me to support their sovereignty claims and keep sending me gifts—Russian caviar, Canadian tires and Danish Danish. But the North Pole has been in my family forever, for goodness sakes. I should have registered my claim centuries ago and renamed it Santaland. But who knew anyone would ever want this place? I'm still not sure why they do, given the changing climate up here.

The North Pole ice is melting and causing me endless problems—from a flooded basement in Santa's Workshop to my leaking polar cap roof. If this warm weather continues I may have to consider moving my operations to the South Pole—and switching from reindeer to penguins. That would be so expensive I probably couldn't retire for another 500 years. It looks like Freedom 6500 for me.

Anyways, kids, I'm sorry to be complaining. The good news is that gift orders have tentupled since we started our website. I miss those handwritten letters but so many of you have switched to email, I had to adapt. I've even gotten used to kids wishing me a "sick" Christmas and asking for "wicked" gifts. LOL.

Emails are pouring in by the billions so we may launch an IPO next year and go public on the Christmas stocking market. I've got a Facebook page too, without my picture since Mrs. Claus says my "jolly" shape sets a poor example for kids, given the obesity epidemic. So instead we have a picture of a svelte reindeer (Vixen), while I've gone on a no-plum-pudding diet.

Anyway, it's getting dark here and the weather outside is blowing, while the skies are gently snowing—so it's time for me to go. Wake up, Prancer! Sober up, Blitzen! Put on that fake brown nose, Rudolph! And to all of you, have a Wicked Christmas and a Sick New Year!

Santa@realsanta. np

www.vehiculepress.com